WRITING THE

FANTASY FILM

HEROES AND JOURNEYS
IN ALTERNATE REALITIES

SABLE JAK

Published by Michael Wiese Productions
11288 Ventura Blvd, Suite 621
Studio City CA 91604
Tel. (818) 379-8799
Fax (818) 986-3408
mw@mwp.com
www.mwp.com

Cover Design: Johnny Ink
Illustration: Robert Winward
Layout: Gina Mansfield
Editor: Arthur G. Insana

Printed by McNaughton & Gunn, Inc., Saline, Michigan
Manufactured in the United States of America

Library of Congress Cataloging-in-Publication Data
Jak, Sable, 1948-
  Writing the fantasy film : heroes and journeys in alternate realities
/ Sable Jak.
       p. cm.
  Includes bibliographical references.
  ISBN 0-941188-96-5
  1. Motion picture authorship--Vocational guidance. 2. Motion picture
plays--Technique. 3. Fantasy films. I. Title.
  PN1996.J34 2004
  808.2'3--dc22
                                        2004004858

Sabl

it br

blue

imag

Muc

trove

popu

Fina

myst

Sable jak deconstructs the fantasy genre and examines it on
every level, from characters and quests to magic and mystery.
No writer preparing to embark upon the epic journey of writing
a fantasy script should start without this literary talisman.

— Shelly Mellott
Editor, *Scr(i)pt Magazine*

"An awesome resource that helps take the mystery out of writing one of today's most popular film genres. Filled with tips, techniques, examples, and exercises that will fire up the imagination, *Writing the Fantasy Film* leaves no stone — or Stonehenge — unturned in an informative and enlightening guide."

— Marie Jones
Book Reviewer
www.absolutewrite.com

"Sable Jak nails writing for this genre with a fanciful mix of no-nonsense, practical information illuminating the magical conventions of cinema. A must-read for every budding screenwriter who longs to be inspired by his noble craft."

— Michael C. Bradbury
Seattle-based writer and producer

TABLE OF CONTENTS

ACKNOWLEDGEMENTS

I would like to thank my writing group: The Screenplayers (*www.screenplayers.net*) for being so patient, encouraging, and enthusiastic throughout this book-writing process. For several years now we experienced many different ups and downs through the life of our group, including the untimely death of member Mary Case, a special woman, no, a very special gal, whose effervescent spirit buoyed us on.

A special "Thank You" to Jenna Glatzer, editor of *Absolutewrite.com* for giving me my first writing gig.

And an extra special "Thank You" to Paul Dwoskin, owner of Broadway Video and all his employees here in Seattle, Washington for allowing me to check out stacks and stacks of movies, and providing invaluable suggestions! (*www.broadwaymarketvideo.com*).

I cannot express enough my gratitude, delight, and the thrill of having both Irvin Kershner and Professor Lister Matheson provide the Foreword and Introduction for this book. I hope I live up to their confidence.

FOREWORD

All cinema is fantasy. Almost anything that an artist or technician can imagine now can be made manifest. Therefore, it is a perfect medium for revealing inner and outer worlds, no matter how strange and different they are from ours.

Vision is a primary sense and with cinema we can employ it to make the most exotic believable. The audience has come to accept the conventions of cinema as an institute for the reality of its own perceptions and feelings. The extreme compression of time and space is accepted as another aspect of reality. Also, the viewer readily accepts shifting points of view (cuts), the manipulation of perspective, and a world that lives within the constraints of a frame, a flat screen as a window to what appears to be a three-dimensional world. As in music, the progression of images is given a rhythmic pattern that can excite or lull the audience.

It all begins with the written word. The screenwriter imagines an invented world and gives it form... however, what is most important are the characters and their conflicts. Drama, no matter what context the story employs, must have interpersonal conflict: protagonist and antagonist. Without this ingredient, no matter the action, imaginative environment, or scale of the film, there can be no dramatic art. Without characters who create sympathetic resonance in the hearts and minds of an audience, a film will have no substance.

This book is an important text for the critical and analytical screenwriter or anyone else who is serious about the structure and conventions of cinema. It is quite miraculous how a fantasy film can transport an audience to other times, past and future, and to the most exotic of places and invade our conscious in the semi-hypnotic state of cinema.

Irvin Kershner
Director
Star Wars, Episode V: The Empire Strikes Back

INTRODUCTION

The appearance of this book is very timely. The recent, huge successes of films such as *The Lord of the Rings* trilogy, the continuing *Harry Potter* series, and the latest remake of *Peter Pan* have been both popular and critical, further emphasizing the fact that Fantasy appeals to the imagination of a wide audience. This should not be surprising, since Fantasy encompasses a variety of sub-genres and underlies many of the greatest works of literature. It is, therefore, natural that from the time of the earliest moving pictures to the present, there always has been a strong strand of Fantasy films. But, as in most things, 90% of these have unfortunately been dross – stereotypical, tired plots and stock characters awkwardly cobbled together and fit only for viewing with derision and loud guffaws.

Sable Jak offers a useful corrective in the present book, which may be the first designed specifically to deal with writing Fantasy screenplays. It is a clear, straightforward, no-nonsense, practical guide to the subject and offers useful suggestions as to what to do and, just as important, what *not* to do. It will stimulate both beginning and more established writers and, on occasion, help both types to avoid embarrassments. I remember well a (thankfully) failed Hollywood TV series, set in medieval England, that featured a dysfunctional family whose attitudes, accents, and idioms were those of modern California and who sat down to a hearty dinner of turkey and potatoes! This book can help to protect us from such *faux pas* and will assist the thoughtful screenwriter in crafting scripts worthy of the many intelligent fans of Fantasy. Read, ponder, digest, learn, and write!

Lister M. Matheson
Director
The Clarion Science Fiction and Fantasy Writers' Workshop
http://www.msu.edu/~clarion/
Professor of Medieval Studies, Michigan State University

PREFACE

Years ago, while on vacation at the Ballynahinch Estate in Connemara, Co. Galway, Ireland, I explored one of the many paths that twist through the 350-acre estate. Ballynahinch (*http://www.ballynahinch-castle.com*) is a fishing preserve and its quiet trails are far from modern intrusions. It doesn't take long to feel as if you're the only person around for miles. As I walked, I listened to the birds and the rustle of small forest animals when, at a bend ahead of me, I saw an ivy-covered obelisk.

My breath, my heart, and time, itself, slowed. The patches of sunlight around me blurred as birdsong twittered into silence. The wind danced counterpoint to the bubbling water of a small stream nearby, as a sigh in my ears asked, "Finally?"

The red and yellow stone obelisk rose 13 feet above me. My intellect told me it was something that had been put there a long time ago by one of the manor's owners and I had not stumbled into the gateway to another world. But my love for the Fantasy genre blew all reasonable thoughts in different directions and, for that short heartbeat of time, I thought I was experiencing what every Fantasy fan longs to experience: The moment when she finally steps into a story and lives it, not reads it.

Of course, nothing happened. The obelisk was put there by human hands, although when and why I don't know. I never asked anyone about it because I didn't want to know – I liked the mystery. Ballynahinch is the ancestral home of the O'Flaherty Clan, Lords of Cannaught. On an island in the middle of a lake there is a ruined castle. It teases visitors with its silent presence. Donal O'Flaherty is reputed to have built it for his wife, the infamous Gráinne (Grace) O'Malley, Irish pirate queen of the sixteenth century. Is it any wonder my imagination seized that moment on the path and drop-kicked me beyond reality?

I still think about that day now and then. Not only was I ready to step into a world of magic from that very real, sun-dappled forest in West Ireland, I was willing and eager to do so. Such beats the heart of a Fantasy fan.

That happy, anticipatory feeling is the feeling a good Fantasy story should invoke in its reader or viewer. It should be so real that, like a sleeping kitten's breath, you may not be able to see it, but you can feel its soft whisper on your cheek. If you can awake in your audience an eagerness to step into your story and ride its slip-stream away from reality, your script will succeed beyond this world, Middle Earth, and maybe even the third star to the right.

Disclaimer

It may seem odd to have a disclaimer at the beginning of a book, but I feel I must include the following:

Writing the Fantasy Film is not meant for first-time screenwriters. In this book you will not find instructions on proper format, act breaks, debates about the index card method of writing, or lists of agents and production companies to contact once you've completed a script. I assume that you already have this knowledge, or know where you can get it. If you think reading this book will help you bypass Screenwriting 101, please note that you will not find half the information you, as a beginner, need to have in this difficult business of writing for film.

Also, *Writing the Fantasy Film* should not be mistaken as a super-duper-advanced-college-graduate-studies-high-mucky-muck-dissertation on Fantasy as a Literary Form. If that's what you're looking for, I suggest you check with your local universities or community colleges and see what courses they might offer. You can also check with the following organization for educational workshops in Fantasy:
Clarion East at: *http://www.msu.edu/~clarion/* in Michigan; Clarion West at *http://clarionwest.org/Web site/index.html* in Seattle, Washington; or Clarion South at *http://www.clarionsouth.org/*, which is not in the southern United States, but in Queensland, Australia.

The Clarion South Web site describes the Clarion organization: "The Clarion Science Fiction & Fantasy Writers' Workshop is one of the most highly regarded science fiction writing workshops in the world. It was established in 1968 by Robin Scott Wilson at Clarion State College in Pennsylvania. The workshop was modeled on the successful tradition of mutual criticism used at the Milford Science Fiction Writers' Conference for professional SF writers. After a number of years Clarion found a new home at Michigan State University and a second workshop, Clarion West, was founded in Seattle. (The Michigan workshop then became nicknamed "Clarion East.")

Past Clarion tutors have included award-winning Fantasy/Science Fiction writers such as: Roger Zelazny, Ursula Le Guinn, Orson Scott Card, and Harlan Ellison.

This book is primarily for writers of spec scripts or assignment scripts based on someone else's idea. Because of this I should tell you now that I do not take examples from hit movie scripts and use them to illustrate a point. Instead, I have written my own little examples. I have done this because I belong to several writers' Web sites and, inevitably, in chats or threads discussing proper writing, someone will state the following: "Well! I read so-and-so's script and that's the way he did it and his movie was a hit, so that's what I'm going to do."

The statement often comes from a person who has read the published shooting script, not the first draft, and we all know how different those can be. Once you've read my example scenes you should do the following: Throw them away and think for yourself. You're an individual, learn from others and use your knowledge to project your own unique voice.

Does this mean I think you shouldn't read scripts of hit movies? Of course not. You should read them, but just repeat this mantra before each reading: "This script shall expand my view, not limit it."

Writing the Fantasy Film is my attempt to show you the components (stereotypical and otherwise) of Fantasy films so you can avoid the traps of formulaic stories. It does not cover how to adapt your favorite Fantasy book, story, comic strip, role-playing game, etc. If, however, you have been hired to do an adaptation and you think this book might have information you can use, I sincerely hope it fulfills your expectations and I wish you "good writing."

Sable Jak

CHAPTER I

WHAT IS FANTASY?

Fantasy stories have been around for a long, long time. They're also called Myths, Fairy Tales, Legends, and even Tall Tales. Around the mid 1800s, the term "Science Fiction" came into general use. In the late 1800s and early 1900s, Fantasy stories began to be published in magazines that featured Science Fiction, thus the term "Sci-Fi/Fantasy" was born. I don't know who first used it, or the exact date of its birth, but it continues to be used today, although not always by Fantasy and Science Fiction fans. This is because Fantasy fans are not always Science Fiction fans, and vice versa. I like Science Fiction, but I **love** Fantasy, I've loved it ever since the first time, as a child, I heard the words "Once upon a time." (Note: The term "Speculative Fiction" is often used today by people who do not want to type-cast an author as a writer of only Fantasy or only Science Fiction.)

Obviously, if I love written Fantasy stories, I feel the same about the movies, whether they're based on old tales or are new ones written specifically for the screen. I am only one of millions of people who love this genre. It's my opinion that the film industry has not capitalized on Fantasy as much as other genres. Yes, there are many movies produced and distributed on a regular basis, but on a whole, good Fantasy is not done as often as its fans would like. However, that may change.

The current financial, critical, and major award-winning films such as *The Lord of the Rings* trilogy and the *Harry Potter* stories ensure that filmmakers will take a more serious look at the Fantasy genre as a viable cash generator. The success of these movies will also result in the following:

1. There will be many rip-offs.
2. Many of the rip-offs will be bad.
3. Writers unfamiliar with the genre, and eager to cash in on the trend, will say to themselves, "Gee, I can write that."

Unfortunately the majority of those writers who are unfamiliar with the genre and who think they can write Fantasy, can't. Why? Because they haven't got a clue what good Fantasy is, or how good it can be. They don't realize that good Fantasy, let alone great Fantasy, is as hard to write as good comedy, drama, or romance. They think all they need to do is include an hour of special effects, a physically strong hero, and a wizard and *Viola!* They've written a Fantasy. Wrong, wrong, wrong.

Fantasy stories – as most devotees will tell you – are NOT just about special effects, strange people, and flying beasties. The stories are about fully developed characters with human traits (even if they're not human) involved in human dilemmas. Sometimes the stories take place in imaginary realms such as Middle Earth and sometimes they occur in unremarkable neighborhoods down the street, like Josh's in the movie *Big*.

How do you write a good Fantasy script? It's not much different than other good scripts. It should come from your heart. There should be characters the audience can feel for and relate to. Dialogue should be believable. And there should be magic, but not only the fantastic kind. It should be the kind that touches the audience, right down to the toes of their inner child.

In the movie *Legend* the Prince of Darkness is told to woo the heroine, Lily. As writers, you should do the same to your prospective audiences. Woo them, make them want to be part of the story, captivate them to the point where they can feel what the characters are feeling.

What captivates a Fantasy fan? My personal thought on this is: The "More" factor. For me the heroes in Fantasies are always more heroic (although they don't always start out that way), heroines are more beautiful, quests more noble, odds more horrific, creatures (if there are creatures in the story) more wild and, well, love is more pure and the end usually boils down to "happily every after," with no one worrying about who's going to take out the garbage or feed the dragon. In Fantasy, the impossible exists. And for those of us who aspire to the impossible, Fantasy offers us the chance to obtain it, if only for an hour and a half in a darkened theater or a few hours spent curled up with a good book.

Before you try to woo your willing audience, let's take a closer look at the many different types of Fantasy:

The Varieties
To many people the term "Fantasy Fiction" encompasses Fantasy (High Fantasy and Sword & Sorcery), Science Fiction, Horror, Paranormal, and Ghost stories, plus all the sub-genres

therein. I repeat what I said in the beginning of this chapter: To its multitude of fans, Fantasy is Fantasy, Science Fiction is Science Fiction and Horror is Horror. End of subject. Devoted fans of the Paranormal inform me that that, too, is a genre unto itself. These different styles often crisscross paths, run parallel to each other and co-mingle easily into the hybrid stories available today. Obviously there is no lack of opinions on what makes each style unique.

Why is one story a Fantasy and another Science Fiction? The simple explanation is that Fantasy fiction relies on organic magic. Beings (human and otherwise) fabricate something "out of thin air" by speaking a spell, waving a wand, or mixing substances such as plants or animal parts, while chanting over them. Also, strange happenings occur (the boy Josh growing into a man in *Big* after making a wish) for no scientifically provable reason. Fantasy is often based on old legends, myths, and fairy tales.

Science Fiction relies on scientific or technical/mechanical means to create something fantastic; such as time or space travel. Beings (human and alien) create machines from raw materials, not by speaking spells or mixing Earth elements while chanting. Science fiction can also take place in ancient times, in the present, on other worlds, or in the future.

Horror is that which terrifies. It can be psychological, organic, or even scientific, but mostly it just makes you want to scream and run, if you weren't having so much fun.

The main focus of this book is writing the Fantasy script. It may touch on other scripts that cross over or mingle, but will always come back to its roots.

Within the Fantasy genre there are many sub-genres. These often hook unsuspecting "I don't like Fantasy" audience members into liking a movie, despite their supposed disdain. Here are a few of the subs-genres and their corresponding films that captured audiences' hearts. You'll find that I've tried to be specific instead of using more general terms such as "High Fantasy" and "Sword and Sorcery."

Romantic: *Ladyhawke, The Princess Bride, Splash, Practical Magic.*

Epic: *The Lord of the Rings, Star Wars, Crouching Tiger, Hidden Dragon, Scorpion King.*

Dramatic: *Legend, Highlander, It's a Wonderful Life, Field of Dreams, Into the West, The Secret of Roan Inish.*

Comedy/Parody: *Midsummer Night's Dream, The Princess Bride, The Witches, The Addams Family, Harvey, Hook.*

Adventure: *Conan, Dark Crystal, The Lord of the Rings* et al, *Willow,* the remake (with Brendan Fraser) of *The Mummy,* and *The Mummy Returns,* the latest (2004) version of *Peter Pan.*

Mythic: *Hercules, The Thief of Baghdad, Clash of the Titans.*

Fairytales:	Many of the Disney Cartoons, Jean Cocteau's *Beauty and the Beast*, *Snow White, A Tale of Terror* (starring Sigourney Weaver.)
Futuristic:	*Star Wars, The Matrix* (a Science Fiction/Fantasy hybrid.)
Coming of Age/ Children:	*The Indian in the Closet, The Never Ending Story, Big, Mary Poppins, The Borrowers.*
Crime/Mystery:	*The Shadow, Highlander, Pirates of the Caribbean, The Legend of Sleepy Hollow* (current remake.)
Christmas:	All versions of *Miracle on 34th Street*, and *A Christmas Carol, It's A Wonderful Life, Bernard and The Genie.*

Romantic Fantasy

This is your classic "boy-meets-girl-boy-loses-girl-boy-gets-girl-back" type of story. Of course magical situations are what keep them apart.

Ladyhawke (1985, Story by Edward Khmara, Screenplay by Edward Khmara, Michael Thomas, Tom Mankiewicz, and David Peoples, and directed by Richard Donner with Rutger Hauer and Michelle Pfeiffer starring). A corrupt bishop falls in love with the lovely Isabeau. Isabeau, however, is in love with Captain Etienne Navarre. Jealousy drives the bishop to curse the lovers, forcing her to be a hawk by day and human by night and Navarre to be human by day and a wolf by night. Thus they are doomed to never be together as lovers again, until someone finds a way for a day to exist without a night and a night to exist without a day.

Set in 13th century Aquila, *Ladyhawke* has a handsome hero, a courageous heroine, and an evil man misusing his power, plus a couple of fun sidekicks who help them sort everything out.

The Princess Bride (1987, story and screenplay by William Goldman, directed by Rob Reiner and starring Cary Elwes and Robin Wright Penn). A greedy, nasty prince tries to marry the young heroine, Buttercup, against her will. Her long absent, childhood sweetheart Westley comes to rescue her, disguised as a notorious pirate. The two true lovers encounter magic potions, strange beasts, and gentle giants in their struggle to be together.

Ladyhawke has some humor, but the love story is played seriously, while *The Princess Bride* uses a great deal of humor and is more of a romantic comedy. The message of both films, however, is the same: Love conquers all.

Two good reasons for writing Romance Fantasies are:

1. They make good date movies (which can translate into good box office).
2. They can be more intimate and therefore need fewer effects, which means smaller production budgets.

Epic Fantasy

The Lord of the Rings: Fellowship of the Ring; The Lord of the Rings: The Two Towers, and *The Lord of the Rings: The Return of the King,* (2001, 2002, 2003, story by J. R. R. Tolkien, screenplay adaptations by Frances Walsh, Philippa Boyens, Peter Jackson, and Stephen Sinclair (on *Two Towers*), Directed by Peter Jackson, starring Elijah Wood and Viggo Mortensen). These movies, to today's audiences, epitomize the Epic Fantasy. Taken as a whole, the trilogy is a tale of evil spreading across the land, engulfing everyone and everything in its path. The evil is stalled by the lack of one small ring of incredible power. It must be destroyed or the world will be destroyed.

As big and as sweeping as they are, Epic Fantasies have the same basic story – the little guy against the big guy. Overwhelming odds threaten to overpower all that is good and decent and it is up to a small band of unwavering – and oftentimes uncertain – heroes to step forward and save the world.

Epic Fantasies, like action films, tend to attract a male crowd, but if the heroes are handsome and the story compelling (and if there's the spice of a little romance with a handsome prince), women gladly go.

Do be aware, should you choose to write an Epic Fantasy, that it has a built-in drawback: Expense. Despite cost-cutting CGI effects, Epic Fantasies still can be very expensive, since they generally utilize several locations. Further, the casts are large, which exponentially escalates production expenses with more costumes, weapons, props, etc. Well-known Epic Fantasies like *The Lord of the Rings* already have an audience because of the popularity of the books on which they're based. Don't let this stop you from creating your own Epic Fantasy spec script, just understand what you're up against and use that knowledge for inspiration.

Dramatic Fantasies

These Fantasies are played straight and concern the human element. Frank Capra's *It's a Wonderful Life* (1946, short story *The Greatest Gift* by Philip Van Doren Stern, screenplay by Frances Goodrich, Albert Hackett, Frank Capra, Jo Swerling [additional scenes] with uncredited contributions by Michael Wilson, directed by Frank Capra, starring Jimmy Stewart and Donna Reed) has delighted audiences for generations. Although not a hit when it was first released, *Wonderful Life* has become a staple of holiday viewing for many families. Its theme of "one man can make a difference" resonates with people today, especially when the world seems so out of whack.

Legend (1985, story and screenplay by William Hjortsberg, directed by Ridley Scott and starring Tom Cruise, Tim Curry, and Mia Sara). In this mix of love story and drama, a young man must thwart the Prince of Darkness from plunging the world into darkness. The story conveys the message that love conquers all, but its underlying theme is: Trust. Trust in yourself, trust in your feelings, and trust in others. Again, a powerful message for all mankind.

Field of Dreams (1989, book *Shoeless Joe* by W. P. Kinsella, screenplay by Phil Alden Robinson, directed by Phil Alden Robinson, starring Kevin Costner and Amy Madigan). This story of a man whose personal – and unspoken – agony over never reconciling with his father leads him on a magical journey to peace. Very few people haven't experienced the feeling of "if only I'd done such-and-such" when they think of a friend or relative who has passed away.

Dramatic Fantasies, as I said, are about being human. No matter what type of magic exists in the story, a unicorn, a whisper on the wind or a bumbling angel, the reality of the human condition is what moves the story along. These are good date movies, but the stories are strong enough that men can relate to them, and touchy-feely enough for women to enjoy. Because they are somewhat intimate, the budgets can be smaller and the stories often give actors a chance to do some solid work.

For a first-time Fantasy writer a little afraid of the genre, a Dramatic Fantasy could be a good way to ease into it.

Parody/Comedy Fantasies
Comedy is magic in its own right, and movies that use magic as the catalyst to comedy sparkle like the gems many of them are. *The Witches* (1990, book by Roald Dahl, screenplay adaptation by Allan Scott, directed by Nicolas Roeg and starring Anjelica Huston and Jasen Fisher) is a delightfully funny, and slyly empowering film about one little boy's fight against a group of bad witches. Of course, that fight is hindered when he's turned into a very cute little mouse. For me the movie had a "yes, I can, yes, I can" message to it. Lots of laughs, but lots to think about, at the same time.

Harvey (1950, stage play by Mary Chase, screenplay adaptation by Mary Chase, Oscar Brodney and Myles Connolly [uncredited], directed by Henry Koster, starring Jimmy Stewart and Harvey, the invisible six-foot rabbit). It's not hard to understand why the play this delightful movie is based on was awarded a Pulitzer Prize. Your main visible character is a man who tipples a little and converses with a Puca (a mischievous Irish spirit/sprite) who looks like a six-foot tall rabbit and is named Harvey. The unseen Harvey makes folkloric, but astute, observations about the people around him. The comments are then relayed by Elwood (Stewart's character.) There is some question as to whether or not the observations are actually Harvey's or Elwood's until the very end of the movie. It may seem that the movie is a piece of fluff, but, as with all good comedy, there are layers to be discovered.

Comedy is always good at the box office, whether it has magic in it or not. If anything, magic gone wrong can heighten the comedy. If you like writing Comedy, and you want to try Fantasy, this might be the way to go. Comedies are also good date movies and good family movies.

Adventure Fantasies

Who can resist a good action-adventure film with daring heroes and plenty of action? When this type of film is done well it's worth every penny of its ticket price. Stories of heroic heroes, gutsy gals, and sneaky villains are only heightened by the addition of magical machinations.

Although the 1932 version of *The Mummy* (story by Nina Wilcox Putnam and Richard Schayer, screenplay by John Balderston, directed by Karl Freund and starring Boris Karloff) was meant as a horror film, the 1999 version (screenstory by

Stephen Sommers, Lloyd Fonvielle, and Kevin Jarre, screenplay by Stephen Sommers, directed by Stephen Sommers and starring Brendan Fraser and Rachel Weisz) and the 2001 *The Mummy Returns* (written and directed by Stephen Sommers, starring Fraser and Weisz) are both balls-out action-adventure movies that hearken back to the daring-do swashbuckling films popularized by Douglas Fairbanks Sr. and Errol Flynn. Excellent CGI effects, fun stories, characters you like, and actors obviously having a heck of a good time all contribute to the movies' ability to thrill. The *Indiana Jones* and *Star Wars* series kicked off the return of this style and I, for one, can only hope it continues for a long time. Of course I would put *Pirates of the Caribbean* in the same category.

This type of Fantasy's main purpose is to tell a darned good tale and keep you entertained. It can be expensive, but it's both a good date and family movie. Single men will go for the CGI and adventure and women will go for the hero and gutsy heroine.

Mythic Fantasies
From the Inuit story of the Raven to the Greek and Roman Myths, Mythic Fantasies recount ancient stories. Every so often these Fantasies are produced but the genre has not found a huge following, unless you're a fan the of Ray Harryhausen films like *Clash of the Titans* and *Jason and the Argonauts*; which are in a class of their own. I find it a shame that so many wonderful myths from all over the world are rarely done. With the present state of CGI, they could be quite spectacular.

Unfortunately "Toga" movies, as I've often heard Mythic Fantasies called, have the bad rap of being stiffly acted (usually vehicles for busty, but-not-too-talented, actresses, or well-muscled, but-not-too-talented, actors) with effects that are clunky and lacking. These movies have their devotees (I consider them a guilty pleasure) but rarely obtain "blockbuster" status. However, the popularity of the TV series *Hercules* and *Xena, Princess Warrior* may or may not see a revival. The TV shows proved that the characters could have appeal if they were made to cater to modern audiences.

Bollywood's movies, although not in the mainstream of American tastes, often recount ancient Myth.

Fairy Tale Fantasies
Of course, these films are based wholly, or loosely, on well-known Fairy Tales from every culture in the world. What differentiates them from Mythic Fantasies is that they generally concern characters who are not god-like and are intended, most often, to be morality tales. I once had a friend tell me she refused to read Fairy Tales (especially the ones by the Brothers Grimm) to her children because they were so frightening. I don't think she liked my "but that's the point" answer. But, that is the point to these stories — they are meant to teach the consequences of bad behavior.

Fairy Tales, especially animated ones with music, have been popular for a long time — that's why they're done over and over again. Purists would prefer to see the stories told as they were meant to be, but most of the time they're "PCed." The lesson the story is telling remains, but it is not relayed quite so gruesomely as the original tale. The live-action versions are often musicals and star up-and-coming young singer/starlets.

An excellent non-mainstream version of a classic Fairy Tale is *La Belle et la bête* (1946, story adaptation of Jeanne-Marie Leprince de Beaumont's *Beauty and the Beast* by Jean Cocteau, directed by Jean Cocteau and an uncredited René Clément, and starring Jean Marais and Josette Day). The acting style is very staged in contrast to today's more natural film style and may put a few people off. Also the subtitles leave a lot to be desired, but the story is portrayed in a dark and surreal manner, making it not only worthwhile to study, but quite interesting.

The 1997 version of *Snow White, A Tale of Terror* (story by the Bros. Grimm, screenplay by Tom Szollosi and Deborah Serra, directed by Michael Cohn, starring Sigourney Weaver and Sam Neill) is one of the best warnings against jealousy and vanity I've ever seen. The sequence of Ms. Weaver eating stew she believes to be made from Snow White's body will make you squirm.

Adapting a Fairy Tale can be tricky because the stories are so well known. If you're determined to write a spec script based on a famous Fairy Tale, you might want to consider approaching the story in a different manner, such as doing *Snow White* from the dwarves' perspective. Fairy tales have built-in audiences both with adults remembering the stories and movies of their childhood, and children whose parents and teachers have read the stories to them.

Futuristic Fantasies

Normally, you think of stories set in the future as being Science Fiction, but they don't have to be. As there are people actively practicing magic today, why would anyone think there wouldn't be practitioners in the future? I also doubt that stories about long-legged beasties and things that go bump in the night won't be around then, either. I might even go so far as to predict that as long as there will be magical moments no one can explain, there will always be oracles, spiritualists, astrologers, and witches.

Star Wars (1977 written and directed by George Lucas, starring Mark Hamill, Harrison Ford and Carrie Fisher) and all its sequels and prequels may be set in that futuristic-looking galaxy far, far away but strip away the space travel and machines and all the heroes really have to win their battles are their determination, their wits, and the use of "The Force."

"The Force," as Ben Obi-Wan Kanobi tells young Luke Skywalker, is in everything, from the rocks to all living things. It is an energy source that can be manipulated by individuals and can be used for good or evil. That's about as organic a magic as you can get, and it illustrates that magic is magic, no matter if it's used in ancient times, present times, or in the future.

Because there are not many Futuristic Fantasies (I certainly haven't seen many) the field is wide open for writers. These films can be good date and family films, but very expensive to produce. However, if you love futuristic stories and can find a way to integrate elements of Fantasy, there's no reason why you shouldn't give this genre a try.

Coming of Age/Children Fantasy

My favorite, for this sub-genre, is *The Indian in the Cupboard* (1995, novel by Lynne Reid Banks, screenplay by Melissa

Mathison, directed by Frank Oz, starring Hal Scardino and Litefoot). A gentle story, it covers serious issues that all children face at some point in their young lives: learning responsibility, choosing what is right over what you want, and learning how to understand another person.

Big (1988, written by Gary Ross and Anne Spielberg, directed by Penny Marshall, starring Tom Hanks and Elizabeth Perkins) albeit very funny, is also an excellent coming of age story, both for the Tom Hanks character, Josh and the Elizabeth Perkins character Susan.

This type of Fantasy makes an excellent date and family movie, and can often be done on a smaller budget. An inherent danger in the Coming of Age/Children's Fantasy is that its charm can get a little too sugary for some people's tastes. But, we all can do with a spoonful of sugar now and then, can't we?

Crime/Mystery Fantasy

Fantasy partners well with Crime and Mystery. After all, what's more mysterious than a strange and unusual occurrence? The characters immediately are in conflict, one trying to keep the mysterious happening hidden and the other trying to find out what's going on. A simple concept, but with magic adding so much more to it.

I've listed *Highlander* (1986, written by Gregory Widen, screenplay by Gregory Widen, Peter Bellwood, and Larry Ferguson, directed by Russell Mulcahy, starring Christopher Lambert and Sean Connery) under this heading. People are being beheaded and The Highlander, Connor MacLeod, knows what's going on and why. It's up to a young policewoman to find out what he knows. In her investigation she gets drawn into a power struggle between immortals.

The Shadow (1937, 1940, 1994, original stories by Walter B. Gibson [under the name Maxwell Grant] 1994 screenplay by David Koepp, directed by Russell Mulcahy, starring Alec Baldwin, Penelope Ann Miller). I recently watched the 1994 version again and liked it as much this fourth or fifth time around, as I did the first time in the theater. The main fantasy aspect of this movie is Lamont Cranston's (and the villain's) ability to use hypnosis on unsuspecting people near him. Despite the fact that he could make people do anything he wants them to, he only uses his unique powers to fight the bad guys. In the meantime, the city buzzes around him, wondering who this shadowy, mysterious figure is.

And lastly, *Harry Potter and the Sorcerer's Stone* (2001) and *Harry Potter and the Chamber of Secrets* (2002, novels by J.K. Rowling, screenplays by Steve Kloves, directed by Chris Columbus, starring Daniel Radcliffe) are good, old-fashioned children's mysteries delightfully spiced with magic spells, floating ghosts, and fierce beasties. Maybe it's the mystery aspect of the stories, but I find the books and movies are enjoyed equally by Fantasy and non-Fantasy fans.

Mystery Fantasies reach a wide audience and can be dark, or just plain entertaining. The danger in this type of script is in going too far with the magic. You need to focus on the mystery part of the story, allowing the fantasy to add to, rather than overpower, it. Depending on the subject of the mystery (and how grisly or non-grisly it is) this can be a good date movie or a good family film.

Christmas Fantasy

This sub-genre is self-explanatory. It may seem as if these stories are slanted more towards the commerciality of the holiday season, but not always. There is usually (no matter how many remakes you see of *A Christmas Carol*) a true moral tale trying its best to be conveyed. Someone I know once said that all Christmas tales suffer from terminal sappiness. Maybe they do, maybe they don't. Most people don't care. For those of us who love Christmas movies, you can lay the sap on 20-feet deep and the story does not suffer. Christmas stories are meant to be warm fuzzies and frankly, who cares if one or two people would prefer to watch *Lord of the Flies* over *The Miracle of 34th Street?* Let them. It's the holiday season and we can use every warm fuzzy we can get.

After reading my list of sub-genres and the movies I've attributed to them, I'm sure you have a disagreement or two. I can believe it. Remember, I said some stories cross over the genres. To a friend of mine *The Princess Bride* was more of a comedy than a romance and that is what he remembers the most. On the other hand, a female friend loves the "true love" aspect of the movie and it was, for her, a romantic story with comic elements – "Fantasy rom-com."

Each movie listed has something different for every viewer. People who say they "just don't buy it" when it comes to Fantasy often admit they like movies such as *The Princess Bride* or *Big* because the elements of humor, friendship, and teamwork are "real" to them.

Origins

With all these sub-genres, you have to wonder, from where in the world did Fantasy first come? The question contains the answer: The World. Every culture across the globe has stories, legends, and myths. Oral and written history has passed down legends of monsters, fanciful explanations about natural phenomena, Gods, Goddesses, and wise people who commune with nature. Fantasy has walked at the elbow of humanity since the beginning of time.

Modern man often views the ancient myths about Gods and Goddesses as quaint, but who knows, thousands of years from now today's major religions may be myths. As long as there are human beings and as long as we wonder about forces outside our immediate control, there will be Fantasy stories. With a little hope, people will continue to turn those stories into movies.

What They Say

I queried several people in the movie and literary world as to their thoughts about the Fantasy genre and here are a few of the questions, and the answers.

Why do you think Fantasy appeals to people?

Linda Seger, Ph.D.: Script Consultant and author of: *Creating Unforgettable Characters and Making a Good Script Great.* Dr. Seger was the script consultant on *The Neverending Story.* (*http://lindaseger.com/*)

"I think that fantasy appeals to the most positive, the most hopeful, and the most adventurous part of our selves. It deals with our sense of wonder, and to our feeling for the possible. I particularly like magical realism, such as *Moulin Rouge*, and *The Little Princess* and *Like Water for Chocolate* because these films are so stylish. When done well, it demands that writer and director hit the tone just right, and never veer off. If the film is way over the top, such as *Moulin Rouge*, it must never lose that feeling. That demands a tremendous amount of art and craft, to never let a wrong note or a dissonant mood enter the picture."

Professor Lister Matheson: Director of The Clarion Science Fiction and Fantasy Writers' Workshop *http://www.msu.edu/~clarion/*. Professor of Medieval Studies, Michigan State University.

"There are various reasons, depending on the kind of person involved. Some like fantasy simply for its escapist quality – they can forget their own lives for a while and live in a different world and even body. More complex are those who see basic human values and issues being addressed in Fantasy, but without all the humdrum events of 'real' life in modern times. It's a kind of stripped-down version of reality, similar to Folk and Fairy Tales, reduced to the big and important issues, including some that are often considered a bit old fashioned these days – honor, heroism, duty, elemental and spiritual forces in the universe, and so on.

Darragh Metzger: Author of the Fantasy novels: *The Strawberry Roan* and *The Triads of Tir Na n-Og* series (Windstorm Creative, Ltd., *http://www.windstormcreative.com*) Ms. Metzger is also a co-director and performer with The Seattle Knights.

"I don't think there is one answer to this question; there are as many answers as there are people who read and enjoy Fantasy. For some, Fantasy is pure escapism, something so totally unlike their everyday existences that it literally takes them out of themselves and away from their daily problems. This sort of Fantasy has its place, and is enjoyable, but I think the very best Fantasy touches us on a far deeper level.

Alone of 'genre' fiction, Fantasy has the ability to touch basic, instinctive fears, hopes, dreams and awaken archetypes that live in our deepest core selves. Good Fantasy speaks to something primal in our subconscious. We lose a little of our self-control when we get involved in a good Fantasy story. Things that we shut off or deny in ourselves in our day-to-day lives wake and live within us when we are touched by well-done Fantasy."

Why do you think some people don't like Fantasy at all?

Professor Matheson: "There are always some people with minds of clay!"

Darragh Metzger: "For some, because they lack imagination. For most, though, I think for exactly the reasons stated above. Some of us don't like to see what we keep smothered and hidden from ourselves in our unconscious minds."

An Exercise

You didn't think I'd let you get away without at least a small exercise or two to try, did you? Don't worry, this one should be fun. Get thee to thy video store and rent two movies, one Fantasy and one non-Fantasy. Make sure they are the same basic genre, for instance, the dramatic Western *The Magnificent Seven* and the dramatic Fantasy *Dragonheart*.

While you watch, keep track of similarities in storyline, characters, and character arcs. Pick fantasy moments that correspond with reality moments and reality moments that seem almost magical. The purpose of this exercise is to show you how similar the stories really are.

CHAPTER 2

RESEARCH,
OR,
IT'S NOT ALL IN YOUR HEAD

No matter what you write about, research is inevitable. How much you do depends a lot on the following:

1. Your subject matter.
2. How much information you feel you need.
3. How much time you can spend on research.
4. How much you do, or don't, love doing the research.

Subject Matter
Fantasy, like any other subject, is the sum total of its parts. You don't write a story about a forensics expert without researching crime, from the types of crime committed to the methods of investigation. Yes, production companies hire expert crime consultants, but you still should have your facts straight in your script so you don't compromise believability. It's the same with Fantasy.

How do you write Fantasy when so much of it is imaginary? Start first with learning about the genre. There is a great deal of information written about it, much more than you think. Where you look for information, and what type of information you'll need, depends on the story you're writing. Is it a romance, a comedy, or an epic tale? I suggest you start where I started:

The Reference Guide to Science Fiction, Fantasy and Horror by Michael Burgess, California State University, San Bernardino. The latest edition (2002) will set you back $75.00 or you can use the your library's copy. In the Seattle library system (where I am) this is a reference book and you can't check it out. I work late into the night, when the library isn't open. Not being able to check out a book doesn't work for me. So I went on the Internet and found a used 1992 edition (out of print) for a low price. This way I can use the library's newer edition when I'm there, and the older one at home when I'm working late. In both editions you'll find listings of encyclopedias, dictionaries, atlases, cataloging guides, awards lists, anthology indexes, artists, authors, movie catalogues, and more. Burgess provides evaluations of all the sources he lists, including the 20 Web sites added in the 2002 edition. These evaluations should give you a chance to focus your search for information. *The Guide* was a valuable tool for researching this book. I only know of the two editions, 1992 and 2002. You'll find an in-depth review posted on Amazon by *Booklist*, the review journal of the American Library Association.

Another book I suggest is *The Writer's Complete Fantasy Reference* by Writer's Digest Books. Each chapter gives a broad overview of different subjects important to the Fantasy genre — from Magic to Traditional Fantasy Cultures — and suggests additional reference materials to assist in your research. First published in 1998 (I have the 2001 paperback edition) the information contained in it (World Cultures, Witchcraft, Pagan Paths, and Arms, Armor, and Armies) is solid and timeless.

Thirdly, *How to Write Tales of Horror, Fantasy & Science Fiction*, another Writer's Digest book, provides a series of chapters written by different popular Science Fiction, Fantasy, and Horror authors such as Ray Bradbury and Marion Zimmer Bradley. The chapters are not necessarily "how-to" information but contain authors' comments on specific subjects such as: "Creating Fantasy Folk" or "Keeping the Reader on the Edge of His Seat." It is an interesting book that provides a look at how these authors view their craft and gives them a chance to share their processes. Published in 1992, the comments by successful authors are not a waste of your research time.

As overview books, these three are good choices, with Michael Burgess' book providing an excellent key to more reference sources.

Of course, many people today hop on the Internet and start surfing around when they need to do research. Before you do that, let me give you these numbers: I entered the key words "Sci-Fi/Fantasy Writing" into Google and pulled up 52,800 sites. The key words "Science Fiction/Fantasy" swelled the number of sites to 1,090,000 and "Sci-Fi/Fantasy Fiction" hauled up 233,000. Entering the same key words at three-day intervals saw dramatic changes in the number of sites. Sci-Fi/Fantasy Fiction jumped from 213,000 to 233,000 in four days. Forgive the understatement, but that's a lot of information on a subject that's supposedly straight from the imagination.

As a cautionary note, if you type "Fantasy" into your search engine, be aware (if you aren't already) that you'll pull up what may seem like a gazillion pages of porn. Once, at my favorite

Internet café, I typed "Excalibur" into Google (I was looking for information on the automobile, not the sword). My embarrassment was compounded by the stares I received from other patrons after my startled bleat of, "Oh my GAWD!"

Obviously surfing the Internet is a case of surfer-be-aware and because of this (forgive me if I sound like your mother), double-check your information when you find it. As you already are aware, there is as much misinformation on the Web as there is good.

If you are fortunate enough to have, in your area, historic researchgroups, such as the Society for Creative Anachronism (*www.sca.org*), their group members can provide a great deal of help in your research. The Society's Web site gives this description of itself: "The Society for Creative Anachronism (SCA) is an international organization dedicated to researching and recreating pre-17th-century European history."

Another cautionary note: Society people are very serious about their historical research. If you go to them asking for "Fantasy" help, chances are you might be rebuffed. They are as serious as any Civil War re-enactment group or other historical society. However, if your script takes place within the time periods they research and you are seeking information to make the "real" aspects of your script as authentic as possible, you will find the help you seek.

The Pacific Northwest hosts several historic/role-playing groups including The Seattle Knights (*www.seattleknights.com*) The Seattle Knights are a combat performance group specializing in medieval jousting and steel combat (yes, real swords.) They put on shows throughout the region and have an "Academy of Medieval Combat Choreography." There you can learn historical fighting techniques and weapons. This, also, is a serious group with certified instructors and members very knowledgeable in their chosen fields.

Another study group in the Pacific Northwest is the Camlann Medieval Association (*www.camlann.org*) that maintains the Camlann Medieval Village in Carnation, Washington. Camlann's brochures state that it is "... a center for the study, interpretation, and enjoyment of medieval culture, that re-creates the every-day experience of a 14th century rural village typical of Somerset, England." It is named after the area where Arthur and his son Mordred supposedly perished. The village's Web site offers links to other medieval Web sites, including the official Web site of the Vatican: *http://www.vatican.va.*

If you're not sure if there are any such groups in your area, magazines such as Renaissance Magazine (*www.renaissancemagazine.com*) often contain listings of different groups and activities. Although members of these groups may not be studying what you are researching, they may be able to assist you. I suggest, if you do look into any of the organizations, that you attend one or two of their functions. Not only will you have fun, but the experience could give you a little bit of a "feel" for your subject.

Lastly, when looking for information on writing Fantasy do not forget about Clarion East, West and South (see the Introduction.) If you're wondering why I have not mentioned the Science Fiction and Fantasy Writers of America, Inc. (*www.sfwa.org*) it is because I have tried to contact them several times regarding this book and have never received an answer.

Okay, I've given you some teaser information on where to find a LOT of information about the subject of Fantasy itself, but what about the components of the genre? Where in the world do you find information about how to create a new world? First ask yourself this: What is the world you want to create like? If you say it's different than anything we've ever known, think again.

Any movie you've ever seen that takes place in another world has similarities to what we know, whether it is the taverns on Tatooine or the farm carts used in the Shire. What is true in real life is true in Fantasy: There are those in power and those who aren't. There is usually some form of music, dance, and art. Commerce exists, as do methods of record keeping. And there are, most definitely, accepted behaviors and moral codes.

If you want to create another world, but aren't sure where to start, research a culture here on Earth that could resemble the world you're seeking to create. It doesn't matter if you pick the ancient Babylonians or the North American Inuits, you'll be able to find plenty of information from a variety of historical, archeological, and anthropological books and magazines. A few of the magazines you might want to explore are: *Archaeology Magazine*, *British Archaeology*, *Egyptian Archeology*, *Discover Archeology* and, of course, *National Geographic*. Even magazines such as *Renaissance* can be of help. If you want to study other worlds writers have made up, get a copy of *The Dictionary of Imaginary Places* by Alberto

Manguel and Gianni Guadalupi. With over 1,200 imaginary places to peruse, you're sure to find inspiration.

If the smallest portion of a myth or a legend is a component in your story, you'll definitely want to look into Joseph Campbell's collected works, if you haven't already. There is no praise I can offer regarding Campbell that hasn't been given before, but I will say this: If you have a limited amount of time for research and you don't know if you'll be able to settle in and study Campbell the way he should be studied, rent, borrow, or buy the wonderful 1988 PBS interview series between Bill Moyers and Campbell, *Joseph Campbell and the Power of Myth*. It is six hours long and absolutely fascinating.

Two other sources you'll want to check regarding mythology are, of course, *Bulfinch's Mythology* and a favorite of mine, *Mythology, the Illustrated Anthology of World Myth and Storytelling*.

Maybe you're not basing your story on an ancient myth, but there are religious figures in it such as monks (*Dragonheart, Ladyhawke*) gods and goddesses (*Clash of the Titans* and the mini-series *Merlin*) or witches, oracles, and vestal virgins. Many Fantasies hint at psuedo Christian/Pagan religions when a story is placed in a Middle European setting. Fantasies in the southern United States, the Caribbean, South America or Africa may include tidbits of the many different forms of voodoo that exist. If you want a religious rite in the story but are unsure where to look try *Ye Gods!* by Anne S. Baumgartner. The book is billed as a "comprehensive dictionary of the gods, from Abaasy (of the Yakut tribe) to Zvoruna (Lithuanian goddess of the hunt)." *Ye*

Gods! is another overview book and does not give a complete history of the various gods or the methods of worship that were practiced in their honor. But, its 201 pages will certainly provide you with enough information about a deity so you can research him/her further. Who knows? Maybe it will spark your imagination enough to come up with a rite that deviates from that overdone scene of half-naked-girls-and-guys-dancing-around-a-raging-fire.

As to researching magic... There is so much information available on the subject of magic you could spend a lifetime researching it, and some people have. I'll be going into more detail about magic and its use in Chapter Seven, so there's no need to cover it here.

Many of the elements of the Fantasy genre are covered in upcoming chapters. The preceding should give you a good idea of how much information is readily available and where you can find it.

How Much Information Do You Feel You Need?

As you've seen, every part of a Fantasy story, from costume to morals, is easy to research. So much so that you could find yourself floundering in pages and pages of information, articles, and notes. Do yourself a favor and try to stick only to the information important to your story. If your characters are watching a pair of amorous Blue Footed Boobies you don't have to put in all the details of the mating dance, just say: "Jack and Jill watch the Blue Footed Boobies do the mating dance." There's no reason to go deeper into your research, unless, of course, you're really interested. Which can present a problem.

I often find that when a subject ceases to be a piece of the informational puzzle and becomes, instead, very interesting to me, I end up wasting time in research, which is disastrous if I have a deadline. (It's only a waste of time at the moment!) To avoid this, keep your research to a "need to know" basis. If it is crucial to your story to find out which foot the Blue Footed Booby dances on in his mating ritual, don't get distracted as to anatomical reasons for it, no matter how interesting they are. You're writing a script, not a documentary with diagrams.

I personally love encyclopedias. They give you the main thrust of what you need to know and from there you can decide whether or not to dig deeper. Fortunately, there are many Fantasy-specific encyclopedias available, such as the ones I mentioned earlier or others like *Encyclopedia of Black Magic, The Encyclopedia of Superstitions* or even the *Encyclopedia Mysteriosa,* which is actually about Mysteries, but does contain information on Science Fiction Mysteries. If there's a Fantasy subject, chances are good there will be an encyclopedia about it.

One of my favorite online encyclopedias is: Wikipedia, (home page: *http://en.wikipedia.org,* Fantasy home page: *http://en.wikipedia.org/wiki/Fantasy+fiction*) but I have a word of caution here, too. Wikipedia describes itself as: "… an online open-content encyclopedia, that is, a voluntary association of individuals and groups who are developing a common resource of human knowledge. Its structure allows any individual with an Internet connection and World Wide Web browser to alter the content found here." The information I found on the site was in keeping with other information I'd researched, at the time I looked at it. So, as with every other site, it's always good

(I repeat myself) to double-check what you've found. What I particularly liked at Wikipedia was its partial list of Fantasy authors. All-in-all, there should be enough information to point you in more research directions.

It's hard to know exactly what you will or won't need for your story. Oftentimes, little tidbits of information (like a knotted red thread is used to ward off the evil eye) are just too juicy to pass up, but you're not sure where to use them. When I research I keep a diary of miscellaneous, but interesting, information and record where I found it. This way, when I'm writing, I can refer back to my diary. (The red thread information is found in many books, but I got it from *The Encyclopedia of Superstitions*.)

One of your goals when you write Fantasy is to make your story as believable as possible. Research can serve that purpose in two ways:

1. It will provide correct information where needed.
2. It will eliminate guess work when you're trying to decide if what you're writing is plausible or not.

How Much Time Can You Spend on Research?
How Much You Do, or Don't, Love Doing the Research.
Obviously, if you have a deadline (whether your own or from an assignment) you need to portion out your research time. With hope, the few materials I've mentioned should give you the idea that Fantasy research could be more labor intensive than you thought, so plan ahead accordingly. The last thing you want to do is find yourself typing with one hand and turning the pages of a research book with the other.

If you love research you could be in big trouble. Fantasy, and all its derivatives, is very, VERY interesting, especially if you're the type who likes to dig up odd little bits of information. You definitely want to take this into account when you're planning your research schedule. Here's a suggestion. Allow yourself time to get distracted; after all, what fun is research if you can't indulge in it a little? Just remember to stay focused and you'll do fine.

What They Say
What movies, scripts, or books do you think a first-time Fantasy scriptwriter should look into to understand the genre?

Professor Matheson:
"I'm tempted to say, 'Avoid Tolkien at all costs' — because he's so good that he could become an overshadowing influence. There are plenty of bad Tolkien-clones about! But Tolkien is the best and most complex Fantasy writer — so read him and be wary of his influence. The best way to familiarize oneself with the genre is to read everything, from the Greek and Roman classics (*The Odyssey*, and *The Aeneid* are, after all, full of the fantastic) to Anglo-Saxon (*Beowulf* has monsters and dragons and a hero who is stronger and smarter than *Conan the Barbarian*) to medieval romances (full of daring-do and adventures) to Swift's *Gulliver's Travels* (strange new worlds, indeed) to Tolkien (the modern master, so read all his books) to present writers offered through the Science Fiction Book Club. There are books on how to write Science Fiction and Fantasy by Damon Knight, Stephen King, Cory Doctorow, Gary Westfahl, Darrell Schweitzer, and John M. Ford that are well worth reading. And, of course, the aspiring writer can attend the world famous

Clarion Science Fiction and Fantasy Writers' Workshop, which has produced so many fine genre writers!"

An Exercise

This isn't really an exercise, but more a bit of fun. I don't know if you're in the middle of writing a Fantasy script at this time or if you're just thinking about it. Either way, schedule an hour or two to go to the library or get on the Internet and compile a list of Fantasy reference books. Include everything you can on the list, from books about other worlds to lists of Fantasy films. Chances are some of the books will point you toward other books and those books will point you to more, etc., etc., etc. You will find that, although you were wondering, at the beginning of this chapter, how to research Fantasy, you now will have so many research leads you'll wonder which one to follow first.

CHAPTER 3

THE STORY
PART ONE

Before we get into Chapter 4, which is all about the characters in Fantasy stories, I wanted to say a little something about story. I know, I know, Character should come before Story! It's an unwritten writing rule that normally should be followed.

If you're reading this book it's quite possible you've got an idea for a Fantasy script. Did I just say, "You've got an idea for a Fantasy Character," or did I say, "You've got an idea for a Fantasy Script?"

When most writers say they want to write a Fantasy, they say, "I'd like to try a Fantasy." Rarely have I heard them say, "I have this idea for a guy who gets caught in a battle between a witch and a wizard." After someone expresses an interest in Fantasy, the conversation usually goes something like this:

Writer: "I think I'd like to try a Fantasy script for a change."

Me: "What kind of Fantasy?"

Writer: "Huh? Oh, well, you know, a Fantasy! Magic, the fight between good and evil, maybe a flying horse, something like that."

Me: "What about the characters?"

Writer: "Well, uh, yeah, there'd be a hero type, maybe a side-kick and a pretty girl." (Writer gets thoughtful look on face, then gets excited.) "Yeah! It could be in this really cool world where everything is in shades of purple and the animals are all people eaters. And the rocks talk. And, and birds are made of a stone-like substance that's light enough so they can fly!"

Me: "What's the hero like?"

Writer: "He's a hero, what else? It's the world that's cool. I can just see it!"

Good. See that world. Envision it. Revel in it. Forget that idiot in the corner repeating over and over, "What's the hero like?" Go on with your ideas, make your notes, decide on your location and yes, even the story line. Your characters will come forth as you need them.

Like I said, this is the shortest chapter in the book because all I really wanted to do was assure you that it is absolutely, positively, and totally okay to come up with your story line first, at least in my opinion.

An Exercise

Grab a cup of coffee and a pad of paper and write down your Fantasy story ideas. If they start out with characters, fine, if they don't, that's fine too. Allow yourself to start out any way you want, whether it's character or story first and go from there. Remember: Fantasy is Freedom.

CHAPTER 4

CHARACTERS

Before we examine your stock Fantasy characters I have a little piece of advice to pass on. There is a book you must, yes MUST, read: *Reel People, Finding Ourselves in the Movies* by Howard M. Gluss, Ph.D. with Scott Edward Smith. Dr. Gluss is a psychologist in California and serves as a consultant to the film and television industries. He holds degrees in Psychology, Communications Studies, and Drama.

I reviewed *Reel People* for *Scr(i)pt Magazine* and afterward gave copies of it to actor friends. Gluss' juxtaposition of real people with "reel" people is an incredible, valuable tool for writers, actors, and directors to help them understand the different personalities people possess and therefore transfer them to characters with whom they're working.

If you've been worrying about how to create a character for a Fantasy story, stop it. Characters in Fantasy stories are the same as characters in other stories. They love, they hate, they are emotional or emotionless. They're plagued by self-doubt and misplaced bravado; they can be greedy, grasping, and nasty, or sweet, adorable, and endearing. It doesn't matter how big or small they are, if they can turn people into toads, or even if they look like you on your worst bad-hair day. The characters in Fantasy are people. Fix that thought in your mind and you should do okay when you create them. A lot of people say Fantasy characters are archetypes. I agree and disagree; it depends on how well they're written.

One attribute of Fantasy that attracts me, and many other women, is the fact that it is filled with smart, strong females, both in lead and supporting roles. The stories aren't always about damsels in distress. Which is not to say that damsels can't be in distress, it's just that quite often they are either very pro-active in their rescue or, after a period of weakness, develop a backbone stronger than dwarvian steel.

As to any special rules that apply to the physical make up of characters in Fantasy, I know of none. They can be anything; human, elfin, dwarves, and even big, fuzzy blue monsters. However, don't think because your character has two heads and belches blue fire, he's interesting. That only makes him a curiosity. What really makes him interesting is the "person" behind the physical facade and behavior, the same as any other hero in any other genre.

Let's examine some of the main characters found in a Fantasy:

The Hero's Hero

Clear of eye, square of jaw, and strong of arm. That's our guy. Usually seen in action/adventure stories, he can fight his way through anyone and anything, from a legion of wraiths to a platoon of storm troopers. He is gentle to little kittens and kind to old ladies (until he finds out they are evil sorceresses). He's often the type of man women love and men want to be. He's rarely disliked by anyone except the villain. In short, he's hell on a sword hilt to bad guys of all kinds and he has, in his most stereotypical form, one basic purpose: To save the day, usually with brute force. It should be no surprise that the hero's hero is not always the real hero of the story. Even if he's smart and clever, he still ends up as the brawn behind the Everyman Hero.

The hero's hero rarely, if ever, has magical powers. Instead he has exceptional physical skills, i.e., he's an excellent swordsman or has great strength. If he does possess magical skills he's usually loath to use them, unless pressed beyond endurance or to save someone else. Sometimes he is given a magical skill but because he's never used magic he tends to botch up what he's doing.

Aside from feats of daring-do, the hero's hero performs a great many other functions in a film. He instills hope and confidence in the weaker members of the story, or an understanding ear to those confessing their fears. On occasion he is the comic relief. He can have a phobia (Indiana Jones and his snakes) that hopefully produces a laugh or two, or he doesn't see the full picture and blunders into silly situations. Sometimes he's just plain shy on gray matter. Strong dramatic undertones can be added to his personality. He can be burned-out, world-weary, angst-ridden, haunted, hunted, egocentric, self-effacing, henpecked, and even high-maintenance (for the comic moments.) With all these possibilities available for a personality background, there is no reason an author can't create a multi-dimensional hero's hero.

One of my favorite hero's hero is Inigo Montoya (Mandy Patinkin) in *The Princess Bride*. He has trained all his life to avenge his father's death and is now a master swordsman.

However, obtaining this status means he has no family of his own, he aligns himself with unsavory characters, and he loves to show off his swordplay. He is pragmatic, values his friends, has a strong sense of what is right and wrong (although he doesn't always pay attention to it) and, like the other characters in the movie, admires and respects true love. As much as Inigo struts around, he is a decent human being. His comedic side makes him a delight to watch, and his devotion to his father makes him someone we can understand.

A very popular hero's hero now is Aragorn (Viggo Mortensen,) from *The Lord of the Rings*. Here is a haunted individual if ever there was one. He loves, he feels, he grieves. He meets danger head-on and is willing to lay down his life to save others. He possesses, in addition to all the basic physical requirements of being the hero's hero, the ability to think things through carefully so he can "walk away and fight another day." He also instills hope in others, although suffers brief bouts of hopelessness himself.

Captain Navarre, so ably played by Rutger Hauer in *Ladyhawke* is handsome, strong, and chivalrous. He is so very much in love with the beautiful Isabeau (Michelle Pfieffer) it is downright tactile to the viewer. Their impossible situation produces such intense anguish you can't help but relate to him, for who among us has not known the despair of a doomed love affair?

Val Kilmer's Madmartigan in *Willow* is pure sword swinging, full-of-himself bravado. A hero in his own mind, this bad-boy-good-guy struts and preens and brags, and then lives up to his own hype. At the same time, when you finally get past the bravado you find he does have a softer side (even though he tries to cover it up) and you realize he's a nice guy, after all.

Of the four roles listed, Madmartigan is the closest to the caricature of the hero's hero. Within the confines of this story, it works and Kilmer pulls it off. It is unfortunate, however, that in many movies, the heroes' heroes are sometimes played by wooden — albeit popular — stars and end up being the ultimate stereotypes.

As the writer it is your responsibility to give your hero's hero more than just a clear eye, strong arm, and square jaw. Your script will be all the better for it.

The Heroine's Heroine

Not seen very often, this character does exist. You could say that women such as *Xena* and *Red Sonja* come close. I find it interesting that writers treat the feminine version of the hero's hero differently. Rarely is she the comic relief, and most of the time she's very smart. Yes, she can be burned-out, haunted, and searching, but she is warmer (albeit, unwilling to show that at first), more willing to bond with someone, and generally not very susceptible to every guy who casts a romantic eye her way. If anything, she usually ignores, or negates, them. I've also found that she has less ego than her male counterpart.

When writing the heroine's heroine it is important to avoid making her a hero's hero with boobs. Yes, she can be a terrific swordswoman or handle an M-16 like she was born with it in her hands, but she still should have a degree of femininity.

The Everyman Hero

One look at real-life heroes and you realize they are simply normal people singled out by extraordinary circumstances. Where the hero's hero is sometimes a one- or two-dimensional person, the everyman is more fully developed from the beginning. He has problems, needs, wants, fears, and joys. He may be a family man as is Willow (Warwick Davis) in *Willow* or a young boy like Josh (Tom Hanks) in *Big*. Sometimes he'll rise to a challenge, and sometimes, he'll be pushed or pulled into it.

The everyman hero doesn't have to be tall and strong, or know how to fight. He doesn't have to be young, handsome, or even human. People around him tend to think of him as a "most likely NOT to succeed" candidate. As much as he tries to stay out of trouble, it will find him.

He may, or may not, have magical powers, but if he does it's possible he wants to keep them hidden because they make him different from his friends and family. On the other hand, he may want to strengthen them instead. There is also the possibility that he is unaware of any special powers until circumstances reveal them.

Some of Fantasy's favorite everyman heroes are: Frodo Baggins, a short, hairy-footed little Hobbit with a little sense of adventure; Harry Potter, a young, rather mild-mannered wizard-in-training; Luke Skywalker, a young man eager and willing to blindly rush in and avenge his dead family; and Mouse, a young thief on the lamb from the authorities in *Ladyhawke*. The everyman hero covers a wide range of types. If you notice, these fellows are drawn into their hero status; they don't actively seek it out.

Luke Skywalker does dream of the thrill of the fight and some glory, but not the kind he's eventually faced with.

The everyman is the epitome of the cliché "still waters run deep." When all seems lost and everyone around him gives up in despair, this little guy manages to dredge up the chutzpah to save the day. Playwright Parke Godwin says it best in the one-act play *Cold Journey in the Dark*. During a conversation between the ghosts of Jesus and Judas (in the present day) Judas tries to explain to Jesus why he did what he did and says: "… it's always a little man who bears the knife, squeezes a trigger, betrays, informs — has HIS hand for one moment closest to the lever and the fleeting courage to pull it." How true this statement is, for heroes are often the little guys who happen to be in the right place at the right time and act, not because of bravado, but because it seems like the right thing to do.

When teamed with the hero's hero, as the everyman often is, not much is expected of him. Consider Frodo (Elijah Wood) in *The Lord of the Rings* trilogy. The fact that he carries the ring of power proves a certain strength in him, but his fortitude is a constant surprise to the members of the Fellowship. Willow also carries an important object, the baby Princess Elora. Willow's determination and strength is a constant surprise to the people around him. Villains are notoriously bad at underestimating the nerve of the everyman hero. They never expect this little person (whether in stature or in nature) to best them, but best them they do.

The everyman hero is always, and will continue to be, an audience pleaser. Why? Because we recognize so much of ourselves in these characters. Our lives are all about our jobs, our families, our joys, and fears. To see someone like us triumph over impossible odds gives us all hope.

The Everywoman Heroine

Never underestimate the shy gal in the corner. She's more capable of outstanding courage than you can believe, especially if her strong sense of what is right and what is wrong is put to the test.

In *Ever After*, a non-Fantasy Cinderella, you have a feisty little gal (Drew Barrymore) who dreams of a smooth life with few problems. Unfortunately she falls in love with a prince.

I love the scene in which Gypsies catch her and the Prince together. The Gypsies realize they can ransom the Prince but they don't need her, so she's told she can leave with anything she can carry. She marches over to the Prince, squats down, slings him over her shoulder in a fireman's carry and, staggering under his weight, proceeds to head home with him. Who'da thunk?

The everywoman heroine is usually regarded by one and all as being unexceptional, almost a non-entity. She's bossed and pushed and not listened to until she's finally had enough. Then along comes an event that puts her in control and she gets a chance to show what she's really made of.

A trap that should be avoided with the everywoman heroine is the "victim" trap. She may allow herself to be pushed around, or manipulated, but under all that outward compliance the audience needs to see that she is not a victim, she is merely biding her time.

Her magic skills, or lack of them, are the same as the everyman hero. A special note about the everywoman heroine: she may be sweet, she may be innocent but she's never, never dumb. Other characters may consider her dumb, but you and the audience know she's not.

The Reluctant Hero

The reluctant hero provides the writer with a large canvas on which to paint. He can be an everyman hero, a hero's hero or even an anti-hero. He has neither a stock personality nor physicality. He can be timid, sweet, stoic, or a scoundrel. Once involved in the adventure at hand he can be a whiner and a complainer from the moment it starts. However, when he's finally in the thick of it, he's committed, fully. The problem is, how do you get him into the thick of things?

Quite often the reluctant hero is a stranger, passing through town. He's seen someone be victimized or he, himself, is the victim of a crime. He can be trapped with the locals by a natural phenomenon, such as an earthquake, or an unnatural phenomenon, such as a rabid dragon or marauding beastie. But that doesn't matter, what's happening is not his fight and he wants none of it. It isn't that he doesn't care, it's just that he doesn't want to get involved so, like the silent stranger in a classic Western, he'd rather move on, thank you very much, ma'am.

Obviously if he does move on, there is no story, so he has to stay. But why should he? What compelling reason would make him stick around? There are several different possibilities but before we go into them, there is one that can be a trap: Revenge. Sometimes it seems that the only way a reluctant hero can be goaded into action is if his family is murdered, his dog run over, or his best friend dismembered.

In American cinema today, revenge is all too often the primary reason for a hero to act. One would like to think that a true hero is motivated by a nobler reason than "getting even." Remember, in Fantasy the heroes are more heroic, the causes more noble. With this in mind you have to ask yourself: What is noble about revenge?

Here are possibilities other than revenge:

1. The simple realization that he is the only person who can get the job done.
2. Survival, i.e., being dragged into a situation that leaves him no choice but to join in or be killed himself.
3. He helps someone in a bad situation and it quickly escalates into a struggle for survival.
4. He is the catalyst that unleashes an evil that threatens everyone's existence. (There's nothing like a good case of the guilts to get someone moving.)
5. He has a strong sense of right and wrong and someone provides an argument he can't ignore.
6. Destiny or a prophecy, i.e., he is proclaimed "the one." Handle this possibility with care, however, as it is also overused.
7. Love.
   a. His own love interest (including his wife) is in jeopardy.
   b. A single mother who is fighting against the odds needs help.
   c. The daughter of someone who has helped him now needs help.

As you can see, there are a number of reasons for a reluctant hero to get into the action.

A nice twist to remember for the reluctant hero is to start him out as a bit of a bad guy. He's not an full-out anti-hero, just someone who's not a pillar of the community, maybe even the local drunkard, and by some odd happenstance (logical, of course) he finds himself the only person with the ability to save everyone around him.

The Reluctant Heroine

I haven't seen many reluctant heroines at the movies. But then, I haven't seen every Fantasy movie ever made (although it feels like it, sometimes). The character I think comes closest to the reluctant heroine is Sally Owens (Sandra Bullock) in *Practical Magic*. Sally is a witch from a long line of witches, however she yearns to lead a "normal" life. Because of this desire she refuses to use her powers and she forbids her daughters to learn the craft. Her sister hooks up with a very nasty fellow and Sally finds that, in order to save her sister, and a new love, she has to step forward and do battle.

The Anti-Hero

Audiences love their anti-heroes. From Sam Spade to Dirty Harry, the guy who treats men badly and women worse has had an enthusiastic following. Why should the anti-hero in Fantasy be any different?

Although he's not as hard-boiled as some anti-heroes in other genres, Han Solo, (also a bit of a reluctant hero) is a good example of the anti-hero in a Fantasy movie. He distrusts everyone, has bounty hunters on his trail and will do just about anything, for a price. In addition he's disdainful, a smart-ass, and cares nothing for other people's problems. Yet, despite these attitudes, he has qualities about him that make the audience love him. He has a maddening self-confidence in the face of danger and, as much as he denies it, has a sense of honor. Also, when he cares, he cares deeply.

Connor MacLeod is another anti-hero. Sullen, seemingly uncaring about others, sarcastic, and challenging, he is focused on only one thing, his own survival. Until, of course, the reason for his attitude is revealed. Underneath it all he is hiding a river of pain. Being an immortal has made him an outsider, and who can't identify with that? From being the new kid in school to the object of gossip, being the outsider is a lonely business.

Not seen that often in Fantasy films, the anti-hero is popular in written Fantasy fiction. A current favorite is Gerald Tarrant of the *The Coldfire Trilogy* by C. S. Friedman. Considered Science Fiction by some, and Fantasy by others, the three books, *Black Sun Rising, When True Night Falls,* and *Crown of Shadows* center on two men trying to rid their world of a force that feeds off the emotions of people. Tarrant, known as "The Hunter," is undead, a vampire (feeding also on people's fears) who murdered his own family to gain eternal life. Yet, as you read further in the trilogy you see he is a man of mercy, longing, and yes, love.

Another favorite anti-hero in written Fantasy is Elric from Michael Moorcock's *The Elric Saga.* Elric of Melniboné can be a nasty piece of work. An albino, he is sickly, angry, and in cahoots with an evil demon. His intelligence is matched only by his ability to wallow in self-pity. He comes from a line of people who lack sentiment and are cruel. He has a beautiful and mighty sword called Stormbringer. Rather than being a righteous sword, this thing sucks the souls of the people he kills, giving him some of their strength so he can live. Like I said, a rather nasty piece of work. Still, he remains a favorite among Fantasy readers.

To the audience, the anti-hero's all-too-realistic shortcomings are totally forgivable, especially when his repressed code of honor is allowed to blossom.

The Anti-Heroine

Not always the main character in a story, you will, on rare occasions, find the anti-heroine in Fantasy. *Xena, Warrior Princess* and *Red Sonja* come to mind for this character. The same danger that existed with the heroine's heroine exists with this character: Do NOT make her a replica of the male anti-hero with a set of breasts.

She can, and should, operate outside the normal societal parameters for women in her culture, but remain feminine. She can be an outcast by virtue of her own actions, or the actions of others, such as Sally Owens in *Practical Magic*. The anti-heroine can be a woman of independent means and therefore reliant on no one else but herself. Whatever she does, she does it because she wants to.

The Buddy

In Fantasy the buddy, i.e. the hero's friend, is unique in that he can be the same species as the hero, or a totally different species. For instance, in *The Lord of the Rings*, Frodo's buddies are fellow Hobbits, but in *Star Wars* Luke's buddy is R2D2, a robot, and Han's buddy, Chewbacca, is a Wookie, a totally different species.

No matter what the genetic background of the buddy, his function is the same as in all stories. He helps the hero achieve what he must achieve. Along the way, he provides his friend with a sounding board, solace in sad moments, a reason for going on, and tough love when the hero wants to pack it in. On occasion he provides comic relief and (especially if injured or killed) the final straw that goads the hero into doing what he's gotta do. I was once at a movie where the people behind me (tired of an annoying buddy character) had a bet going as to when he would die. Obviously, you want to make your buddy appealing enough that this doesn't happen. To avoid it, simply think of all the qualities you appreciate in your friends and choose the ones you think would be best for your hero's bud.

A buddy should exist ONLY if he's needed. He shouldn't be there just for laughs or to die, or because you think the hero has to have a friend. In *Ladyhawke,* Captain Navarre and Mouse are not "buddies" but two people whose paths cross and they end up traveling together. They form a caring friendship, yes, but they are never really buddies. Samwise Gamgee (Sean Astin) in *The Lord of the Rings* is, however, a buddy. His friendship with Frodo is established from the very beginning of the first movie. As the two travel together, Samwise proves himself to be the very best of buddies.

Another good buddy character is Billy (Jared Rushton) in *Big*. He's Josh's friend and although the two aren't constantly together during the film, he serves as Josh's anchor to his childhood. He's also a little more adult-savvy than Josh and is able to help his friend survive until they can figure out a way to get Josh back to his normal size and age.

Depending on what is required of the buddy, he is usually portrayed as being smaller, less skilled, not as savvy, or, in some way, not as adapt as the hero. Of course, this isn't always true. But you should get the feeling that, in order to survive, the hero needs the buddy as much as the buddy needs the hero.

Because of the hero's trust in the buddy, the writer has ample opportunity for conflict by exposing the buddy to temptations, betrayals, and jealousies; all emotions that factor in the break-up of real-life friendships.

The Magic Person as Mentor
Frodo has Gandalf, Arthur has Merlin. Rand (in *The Wheel of Time* books) has Moiraine Sedai. All these people are mentors and they all possess magical abilities. In addition, they have a great deal of knowledge coupled with common sense. They are also fallible and they always have their limits. Without those limits the magicians wouldn't need heroes to complete tasks, they could complete those tasks themselves. But then where would your story be?

A magician is usually bound by a variety of outside influences that stop him from using magic constantly to save the day. Some of these influences may include:

1. He is losing his ability to perform magic.

2. His instrument of magic — a wand, a staff, or a piece of jewelry — has been: stolen, broken, or rendered impotent. (Authors can have a lot of fun finding ways to decommission the magician's instrument.)

3. He has been imprisoned someplace where magic doesn't exist and therefore his won't work.

4. His powers have been stripped, which is similar to #3, but still a little different.

5. He's under a spell.

Although very common, the magician/hero relationship is not always that of teacher/student or master/apprentice. Sometimes the two would rather not deal with each other at all, but for reasons beyond their control they are forced to work together. Such outside reasons could be:

1. Threats to the local ruler.

2. A kidnapping of someone important.

3. A beast terrorizing the countryside.

4. The two are trapped together.

5. They're related in some way.

Having them thrown together, and not liking each other, gives you instant conflict, plus a paved road to cliché hell, if you're not careful. Your reason for them to be stuck with each other MUST be very good, and very logical, for the story to be fresh and interesting.

What exactly is the function of the magician? It's not always to save the day with a wave of his wand. Well, sometimes yes, but not always. His job is to set the hero on the right path, provide the proper tools to use while on the path and, when he can, offer assistance and sage advice. Of course, if the hero would listen to the advice, use the right tools, and follow the path pointed out to him, we'd have a very short story. Things get interesting when the hero takes off on his own path or if he's forced off it.

Magicians can be: long suffering, impatient, distracted, annoyed, inept (and if they are, they should be VERY inept). They do not HAVE to be all-knowing and all-seeing. Extra life can be added to the relationship if, on occasion, the magician finds he does not have a complete grasp of the situation and he and his charge are in deep trouble. Of course, the realization that the magician is not all-seeing and all-knowing is a turning point for both the hero and the magician and provides the author with a chance to add extra conflict and humanity to the story.

Your magic person can be old, young (maybe a new wizard just learning his trade), a mischievous cricket, or anything you'd like him to be. He can be killed off or not, and, if he does live he quite often gains knowledge and understanding from working with the hero.

The Witch (Bad & Good)
The Bad Witch
She's lean, she's mean, and she's usually ugly. If ever there were a more stereotyped character, I don't know her. At her stereotypical worst she stirs a cauldron, screams and cackles a lot, and gives the impression of raging menopause, no matter

what her age. About the only thing that seems to give her pleasure is baking children and skewering anything pink and fluffy. The classic bad witch is over the top and — for actresses — darned fun to play. At the other end of the spectrum she's lean, she's mean, and drop-dead gorgeous, but just as horrific.

She's lean, she's mean, she's usually ugly. The Witches *(1990)*

A bad witch's reason for being nasty varies. Jealousy, greed, and vanity are often part of her make-up, especially in morality tales. To me she's the true archetype in Fantasy because her badness is rarely questioned, nor is it explained. She's bad and that's all there is to it.

As fun as the bad witch role is for an actress, it's more fun for the audience when there's some depth to her. It doesn't have to be fathoms, just enough to hook them. And here is where the writer can join forces with the director and actor. All it takes is a line or two to give them the information they need to turn this over-the-top villainess from an archetype into a real person. But make sure to keep it simple and maudlin-free.

The Good Witch
Forget Glinda. As nice as she was in her Southern Belle dress and sparkly crown, most good witches tend to have more developed personalities. For starters, they're not weaklings. They can't afford to be. They're too often in conflict with the bad witches and in that type of battle there's no place for weakness. This doesn't mean that they have to win the battle. Good witch Fin Raziel (the late Patricia Hayes) in *Willow* loses her battle with the bad witch (although the day is saved by Willow himself). I liked Fin Raziel. She could be kindly, but she was also bossy and accepted no nonsense, from anyone. Good witches can be anything you want them to be, from a suburban housewife to a maiden aunt with a taste for tequila. That's why I say; if you're going to have a good witch in your story, forget Glinda. Bring on someone who's real.

The Hero's Love Interest
There are four basic Hero's Love Interests:

> True Love
> Evil Love
> Pure Love
> Reluctant Love

True Love

We all know what true love is. It's finding that one soul mate meant for you and you alone. It's holding hands after 90 years of marriage and withstanding everything life throws at you, as long as you withstand it together.

In *The Stairway to Heaven* aka *A Matter of Life and Death* (1946, written by Michael Powell & Emeric Pressburger, directed by same, starring David Niven and Kim Hunter), true love triumphs over death. In this film a young WWII RAF pilot is forced to bail out of his plane over the English Channel. He's returning from a bombing raid in Germany and his parachute has been destroyed. He makes contact with an American radio operator. She is the last person he talks to before he jumps from his burning plane. However, because his guardian angel (the one that was supposed to take him to heaven) gets lost in the thick English fog over the Channel, the young man survives and, of course, when he meets the girl, they fall in love. The Powers that Be in Heaven aren't too happy about the situation and send the angel to get him, but the young man argues that it's not his fault he's not dead and that he should have some sort of right to an appeal.

And therein lies the story. He must argue his case before the Heavenly hosts and prove that his love is, indeed, true love and worth his being allowed to live. There is a political message to the story (as in a great many films of that time period) but it is, overall, a sweet Fantasy (crossing heartily into the Ghost genre) and a delight to watch, as are most true love films.

True loves are willing to give up their own lives for each other. They'll go to hell or any other horrible place in the name of love. In *Legend* Lily tells the Devil she'll marry him if he'll let her kill the Unicorn. All the while she plans on letting it go. She knows this will doom her, but it will mean that Jack, the boy she loves, and everyone else, will be free of the Devil's darkness.

Evil Love

Evil love is, well, evil. It is obsession mistaken for feelings of love. An evil lover doesn't care that the object of her affection can't stand her; she'll do anything to get him. She wants him and that's all she needs. She's also convinced she can change his feelings about her if she can prove her love. She tries over and over again, and when it doesn't work, she gets frustrated and either tries to kill him or the person he loves. Of course, this backfires and usually brings about her demise.

Sometimes she manages to bewitch him with a spell or enchantment. However, once she's enslaved him, she discovers she can't stand him, until his true loves shows up. Then she really goes crazy.

Sometimes the evil love causes a perilous situation for the man with whom she's obsessed and the only way she can save him is to team together with her rival, the hero's real love. It's not unusual, at this point, for the evil love to die saving the hero, providing a poignant moment in the movie when she learns what true love is. Sometimes, however, she doesn't die, learns what true love is, and walks away a better person. The choice is yours.

Pure Love

Pure love is, for the most part, that old standby, unrequited love –
in which the hero worships someone who is untouchable, but
someone for whom he'd die (and occasionally does). Although
not Fantasy films, *Cyrano* and *Casablanca* are good examples.
In Fantasy, the hero (or heroine) often manages to get together
with the person he loves at the end; if not, we'd never be able
to say "happily ever after."

However, sometimes pure love remains unrequited. In
Ladyhawke, Mouse has come to love Isabeau, but because she
loves Navarre (and is Mouse's "better," socially) he is content to
know that she is genuinely fond of him. Jealousy is unknown to
him. He even puts his own life in danger to save her on more
than one occasion.

Of particular note in this story is the fact that the curse surround-
ing Isabeau and Navarre was delivered by an evil (possessive)
love, but the destruction of that curse is helped by the power of
Mouse's pure love.

Reluctant Love

Think of a Fantasy version of *African Queen*. Two people,
thrown together, maybe they don't even like each other, and
after battling dragons, evil witches, nasty beasties, and all manner of misery they just, well, discover they kinda-sorta like each
other, a whole lot, and that "like" turns into love.

In *Willow*, Madmartigan is sprinkled with Brownie love dust
and falls in love with Sorsha (Joanne Whalley), the evil
witch's daughter. He doesn't want to be in love with her and

she is, at first, repulsed by his advances, but slowly, they both come around.

With reluctant love, the trick is to get your opposites to attract, but not do anything about it until the audience is practically howling for them to get together. Of course, that's not the only way to deal with them — they can do the boy-meets-girl-boy-loses-girl routine — but by the end of the movie the chemicals they've been mixing should be exploding.

The Friendly Antagonist

Not all antagonists are nasty. Some of them are along for the ride or the money and aren't necessarily bad guys. Some are scoundrels or a little on the roguish side. They can be charming, foppish, or ladies' men (or flirty wenches, if female.) They can also be gruff, smelly, ugly, grumpy, and complaining. Deep down inside they're really nice guys whose "straight and narrow" sense of self tends to either bend a bit or twist totally around. You could consider Inigo Montoya from *The Princess Bride* a friendly antagonist at the beginning of the movie. Yes, he eventually ends up as a hero, but he gets involved in the adventure for two reasons, one, he needs the money and two, he's looking for the six-fingered man.

The friendly antagonist usually has an ulterior motive. He may have a dastardly background, but, because he's not interested in harming the protagonist, it's forgiven. Jack Sparrow (Johnny Depp) in *Pirates of the Caribbean*, wants his boat back. He's a pirate. He's nasty, he's vile, he's known for killing, looting, pillaging, raping, and who knows what else. But, he actually treats the hero and heroine rather nicely, even to the point of being on their side (if only to get what he wants). Who can fault that?

Obviously, the friendly antagonist lends himself well to a character with humor and panache.

The Temptation-Prone Friend

Nothing like a little temptation to spice up a story. Usually, but not always, this poor person is a buddy. He gets lured away from the main thrust of the hero's quest with any manner of distractions, from a puppy that turns into a friend-eating monster to a shiny bauble that mesmerizes and imprisons him. He's the first to hear the siren's song and quite often the first to wake from her spell.

His age, stature, sex, and species group doesn't matter. If there's a temptation around he's all for checking it out. And that's where the *writer* can get into trouble. Overdo the temptation-prone friend's predilection for trouble and you'll have audiences screaming for him to give in to a deadly temptation, just to rid them of having to watch him bungle things up again.

Quite often, at the end of the movie, it might seem that this fellow (or gal) has been cured of his affliction. Don't bet on it. The last shot of the movie sometimes hints that he'll never give up his ways.

The Evil One

There's nothing as wonderful as a terrific bad guy. Think of The Devil in *Legend* played to perfection by Tim Curry. How could you not like this guy? He has angst. He is big, bawdy, and nasty, and is turning himself inside out to get a bride; all the while plotting to plunge the world into eternal darkness. After all, if the world is going to be in eternal darkness, why not have someone with you while you enjoy it?

Your audience should have one of two reactions to your evil one: They either hate him and can't wait to see him get what he has coming, or they love to hate him, which means they're not too annoyed if he gets away.

An old forensics teacher of mine once said that some people were born bad. He should know, he's caught some of the worst. But modern man has a hard time thinking of someone as being born bad. (That's a debate that should be covered in a different kind of book.) In a screenplay, a bad guy who's bad "just because" makes for one very ho-hum character. The very best evil characters are the ones who have a purpose. Whether it's world domination, obliterating good, resurrecting an old girl-friend, or annihilating anything that's cute and cuddly, a good evildoer has a focus that draws the hero in and actually gives the hero an extra weapon in fighting the bad guy.

Obviously, purposes such as world domination and obliterating good have been done over and over again. So if you feel you must use them, spend additional time thinking up unique thwarting techniques for your hero.

This may sound odd, but a good evil one also has a sense of humor. It's often bizarre, but it is humor, nonetheless. For instance, a bad evil one would kick a puppy and laugh. That doesn't really get the audience on his side. He can slap the good-guy around, but kick a puppy, nah, that's something for an inferior evil one to do. A good evil one would kick the guy who kicked the puppy. He might, later, do something nasty to the puppy; it just depends on how you want your audience to react to him.

Sometimes an evil one has a strange little trait that makes him almost likable. Maybe he actually loves his mother and sends her chocolates on her birthday. Or he likes kittens. He could be a snappy dresser, almost to the point of silliness or he has a weakness for a particular food. Often, that odd little trait can be his downfall.

The evil one can be over-the-top or very subtle. Of course, the final performance of your words will be in the hands of the director and actor, but if the character has multiple dimensions, your audience will be pleased.

The Evil One Wannabe
There are two types of evil one wannabe's: The wretch and the junior executive. And, of course, in between these two there are sub-wannabes. Remember, this is Fantasy, there are no absolutes. Let's examine the two main types:

<u>The Wretch</u>
This poor, pitiful person epitomizes the old saying "always a bridesmaid, never a bride." Try as he might to be a real evil one, he's got everything going against him. Including the fact that he probably doesn't really want to be bad. He's just been picked on so much all his life he's decided he's going to get some of his own and has joined forces with a real evil one. The only problem is, the evil one doesn't look upon it as "joining forces." The wretch is, to him, just another minion to kick around, order about, pick on and, in the end, render expendable. The wretch is right back where he started when the boys at school stole his lunch money and threatened to flush him down whatever medieval crapper happened to be available.

Sometimes you wonder why the evil one keeps the wretch around. He's oftentimes inept, clumsy, not really very evil, and more of a burden than a help. But he also happens to be slavishly devoted, and therein lies his attachment to the evil one. The evil one knows that no matter what he does to him, the poor wretch will be back begging for more; anyone else would have left him long ago.

Usually, the wretch winds up one of three different ways at the end of the story:

1. Dead (the evil one's reaction is varied on this, it depends on how sympathetic you want to make him).
2. Finally getting backbone and turning on his master. (This can be a really juicy scene to write, but remember, brevity!)
3. Alone, after his master has been killed. His own inherent ineptness makes it impossible for him to muddle on by himself and he often fades into the background to seek out another evil one to follow.

The Junior Executive
Yup, he wants the penthouse office. He's sly and slick and often more evil than the evil one; just not as smart. He has come to learn at the knees of the master, and will ultimately burn everyone around him.

He has a small problem, however. He lacks the essential quality that makes him a true evil one: vision. His main focus is on ousting the big guy. Beyond that point he's a little hazy. Sure, he has plans, quite often big plans, but he doesn't realize that the evil one got where he is by a lot of hard work and very careful planning for the future.

The evil one is a little like the gunfighter in the Old West. Once a shooter eliminates everyone above him and is now top man with a gun he becomes the prime target to everyone below him. The evil one has learned this and has developed a keen sense of survival, something junior hasn't worked out, usually.

Personally, I like junior. He can be so much fun to write you almost forget your other characters. So be careful, he can take over a story, which is exactly what he'd like to do anyway. His motivations for being what he is add much to a script. Depending on what you want to do with him, he can be the normal greedy, grasping person people are used to seeing. But that's old and boring. Anyone who's going to try and usurp the evil one has got to have a twist in his knickers someplace! Maybe the evil one stepped on his pet cockroach when he was a child and this is his way of getting back at him, maybe he made a promise to someone, or maybe, if you want to introduce a terrific twist (be sure to foreshadow it), he's a latent good guy who's there to destroy everything the evil one's tried to build. Junior can even be a deep cover spy (yes, there are spies in Fantasy) for the good guy. Heck, he can be motivated by his mother. Don't think so? Does the tag-team of Morgana le Fay and Mordred ring a bell?

Like I said, there's lots and lots of fun to be had with junior. He can have so much depth you'll surprise yourself. But remember; don't let him run the story.

The Captive Magic Maker

This isn't *de rigueur*, but many Fantasy stories have a captive magic person (male or female, maybe even a beastie). He is often the strongest of the strong, mighty and supposedly unshakeable. But he has, somehow, gotten himself captured. Usually, the captive magic maker provides a secondary story. The hero has a task to do and in order to complete it he needs the magic maker, so a rescue must be mounted first. *Willow* uses this device when the heroes are sent to rescue the sorceress Fin Raziel. Sometimes, of course, the thrust of the story is the rescue itself.

Obviously, and especially for those people who don't like Fantasy, the fact that a person has magical abilities raises the question: How the heck did he get caught in the first place? Magic, as I said before, is not limitless, but I'll go into that more in the chapter about magic. Until then, here are a few ideas you could use to capture a magic maker:

1. He's under a spell. No matter how good someone is at his skill, there will always be someone better, so a magic maker falling under a spell isn't a far-fetched idea.
2. A loved one is held captive and can't be reached and to save this person, the magic maker must give himself up.
3. An unholy bargain has been struck and the captive magic maker agrees to provide assistance to the evildoer to avoid a larger disaster. He, of course, knows that his capture is all part of the big picture.
4. He is imprisoned somewhere that prevents his magic from being used.

5. If his magic is related to the spoken word, perhaps he has been gagged or his tongue has been removed.

6. And (my personal favorite), the magic person has been captured by something silly, such as a sly pixie grabbing his wand (or whatever he uses to create magic) as he takes a swim or is otherwise occupied.

Of course, all of the above refers to a good magic maker as a captive. If an evil magic maker is being held you've got a whole new story to tell.

A captive evil magic maker could put the world in jeopardy. Demons, evil wraiths, and vile monsters could walk the Earth searching for him so they can let him loose. Where your heroes were trying to free the magic maker before, now they are trying their best to keep him imprisoned. Of course, the evil magic maker attempts to wield his power on the people holding him. He plants doubts, tries spells, and pits friends against each other. He is the proverbial viper in the nest. What unholy fun.

The Evil One's Love Interest (Willing and Unwilling)

The evil love interest is the main squeeze of the evil one. Or, it could be someone he wants to be his main squeeze, usually against her or his will. Think Buttercup in *Princess Bride* or Lily in *Legend*.

Lily is one of my favorite evil love interests. In *Legend* young Lily, in her innocence, touches a Unicorn. This forbidden action brings forward the Devil's son. Her innocence captivates and fascinates him. His purpose is to snuff out all light in the world by killing the Unicorns. He knows that if he can bring her, and her innocence, to his side he'll be able to do it. In his own, odd, evil way, he falls in love with her and decides to woo her to his side, offering her anything she wants.

At first she's frightened, then she fights him. When that doesn't work, she gives him hope that she might be interested and uses that to provoke him. It drives him into a towering rage. Just when it looks as if he'll kill her, she tells him she'll come over to his side. So delighted is he that he doesn't realize innocence has developed cunning. She tricks him and pulls off a *coup de grace* that would make General Patton salivate.

This little slip of a girl lives up to all the amazing, unwilling evil love interests in Fantasy stories. She takes the meaning of the words "love hurts" to new heights. The easiest trap to fall into when creating the evil one's love interest is to make her beautiful, and stop there. If you've done a good job on your hero and he's a multi-dimensional person, make sure the heroine matches up to him. You don't have to make sure she can swing a mini-broadsword and kick demon butt with the best of them, but make sure she's got brains. Lily was frightened and at first looked like she might fold, but boy, she pulled it together, and so should your heroine.

Now, the *willing* evil love interest has been, for the most part, relegated to the background. She gets a chance to betray people, and mix things up a bit, but basically she is often a stereotype of a naughty girl who's fallen for a bad guy who's forever trying to be in the limelight.

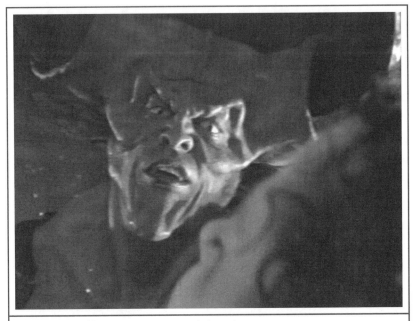

Innocence develops cunning. Legend *(1985)*

What a waste! Make her cunning, not whiney, or make her crafty and not a hanger-on. She can be a helpmate or a rival. She can love him, or she can fool him into thinking she loves him, when she really hates him and is just ingratiating herself to wreak a little of her own havoc.

This character offers you so many opportunities you should be dizzy with delight. Don't waste her (or him) — you'll be glad you didn't.

The Prod
Behind every hero, reluctant and otherwise, is someone willing to walk beside him and help shove him along until he does what he should do. A parent, a lover, a chum, a rival — it could be anyone.

Sometimes the prod is actually disguised as the buddy. He goes along with the hero until the hero starts to falter. He then delivers his St. Crispian's Day speech, calculated to get the hero moving again. Of course, a magician, various love interests, and even the evil one can be the prod, too.

The prod is not always limited to working with the hero. A classic example of an evil one's prod is Morgana La Fay. She brings down her brother Arthur by putting her son, Mordred, into the volatile mix of personalities at Camelot. She's raised him to believe he belongs on Arthur's throne and together they go after it.

When working on a comedy Fantasy, the evil one's prod is often a mother (an over-the-top version of the Morgana/Mordred relationship), an ugly sister, a spouse, or a love interest.

Never look upon the prod as someone who's there "just to move the story along." Within the confines of that movement you should be able to find any manner of delightful methods that veer widely away from the common trails followed by many other writers. This is Fantasy, use your imagination.

The Evil Friend

All fiction (and sometimes real life) is full of relationships that develop between opposites. Often the relationships are based on a mutual respect and nothing more. This ploy is almost cliché in detective stories — on screen and in prose — where the local police Lieutenant has a grudging relationship with a private investigator.

The same type of relationship can exist between an evil one and a hero. For example, the TV series, *Buffy, The Vampire Slayer* uses it.

There are many reasons for an evil one and a hero to co-exist.

1. The two were friends before one became evil. They may have had the same choices, but chose differently. Their past keeps them connected and for some reason the character who turned to evil has not totally abandoned his old friend. It is important to note that the good guy believes that the evil friend will, one day, turn back to being a good person.
2. They have to band together to fight a greater evil. This relationship exists in C. S. Friedman's *The Coldfire Trilogy*.
3. The evil friend owes the hero a favor or vice versa.
4. Or, just for a wild card reason, perhaps they share a love for Celtic music, Abyssinian cats, Cajun cooking or antique maps. It doesn't matter, the more unusual the reason, the more fun the relationship can be. However... if you pick an unusual reason for their being friends, make sure it is a logical one.

On occasion, the evil friend helps out the good guy. He rescues him, passes on pieces of information, maybe gives him a warning. Of course, the good guy will return the favor if he is able and if it doesn't go against his ethics. This type of "scratch-my-back-I'll-scratch-yours" relationship is not unusual, for, despite their own personal codes, they have reached a level of mutual trust in their relationship.

The evil friend can be a truly awful person or being, or he can be charming and disarming. In the vampire-detective TV series *Forever Knight* starring Geraint Wyn Davies as police Detective Nick Knight — first played by Rick Springfield in the 1989 series pilot — Nick is helped quite often by fellow vampires Lacroix (Nigel Bennet) and Jeanette (Deborah Duchene.) The "evil ones" don't like, or understand, Nick's desire to be normal again, but because of past relationships they remain friends. Lacroix is harder edged, while Jeanette is softer. (No, I haven't forgotten the TV series *Angel*, I just elected to go back a little farther.)

It should be noted that the evil friend rarely, if ever, crosses over to the good side. When asked if he'll cross, he usually smiles, says he'll think about it, and then walks into the darkness.

The Comic Relief (Sometimes NOT!)

As I've pointed out with other stock characters, they occasionally can provide the comic relief needed to lighten the mood. Many films, not just Fantasy films, have characters whose function seems to be just that and nothing else. Sometimes it works, sometimes it doesn't. And, sometimes it's not the writer's fault; the characters have been added or changed during pre-production (especially if the writer is no longer involved).

First, let's look at the real comic relief character. Usually he's a bit mischievous, overly curious, and meant to be delightful. In *The Lord of the Rings*, Merry and Pippin accomplish all of this, however they also fight like little heroes when they have to. Their loyalty and affection is never questioned and when pressed, they are capable of intelligent thought and action.

They are comic relief characters at their best. At their worst, however, comic relief characters can be annoying to the point that the audience prays for their demise. Jar Jar Binks from *The Phantom Menace* was hated by just about everyone I know. And, as much as I love the movie *Willow,* I have to admit, sometimes I wished someone would step on the two little Brownie characters. Obviously, you want to avoid this type of reaction.

But how do you avoid it? First, ask yourself what purpose the comic relief serves. Your answer should be: He's supposed to give the audience a brief breather between onslaughts of intense emotion or action. The definitive word in that meaning is "brief." To stop your designated comic relief character from becoming a comic burden, keep his moments in the spotlight short and clean. At all other times let him function as normally as possible. He still can be funny, and even silly, but not in such a way that he steals focus from the action around him.

Another question you should ask yourself while writing is: Does my story really need a comic relief character? If you can disperse comic moments and comments to your other characters — and do it believably — you'll definitely want to drop the comic relief.

The Kid

He, or she, is smart, quick, oftentimes a street urchin, always precocious and gets people into, and out of, trouble. If he isn't an orphan, his beautiful young mother is a widow or he has a gorgeous sister. And, of course, when the kid is caught by the bad guy (and he always is) the hero has to give himself up in order to save him. Be careful when writing this role. It's a difficult stereotype with which to work. One of the best non-stereotypical uses of the kid that I've ever seen is in the Science Fiction movie *Aliens*. She's cute but not precocious, she's ballsy and tough but not mouthy, and best of all, she doesn't steal focus.

Fantasy, like all other genres, has many other stock characters. Bartenders, innkeepers, taxi drivers, smithies, soccer moms, and comely wenches populate the scripts. Include the ones you need only if you NEED them. Remember, every speaking role in a script increases the budget. If a barmaid's wink at the hero conveys her intentions, drop her "ooh, I like your big biceps," line.

I have one last question you should ask yourself when creating your characters. Look at each one carefully and ask: Is this person the best that he can be? If he's not, you know what you have to do.

What They Say
Aside from magical abilities, do you feel the characters in Fantasy are different from those in a non-Fantasy story? If yes, why? If no, why?

Professor Matheson:
"Characters in Fantasy are often simpler than characters who are intended to mirror fully complex, modern characters. This is not necessarily a drawback, though — it allows Fantasy characters (or at least well-drawn ones) to concentrate on the 'big' issues. Again, it's a stripped-down-to-essentials way of looking at human existence (even if the characters involved are non-human!)"

Darragh Metzger:

"That depends entirely upon the Fantasy story, and writer, and the tale being told. In Tolkien, for instance, the characters are all archetypes, or primal manifestations of the very best and the very worst in all of us. They are larger than life, yet few are realistic human beings (with the possible exception of Sam Gamgee). In something like Charles de Lint's urban Fantasy stories, the characters are ordinary people who find themselves encountering the extraordinary — magic and creatures out of Fairy Tales, etc. — and cope with it as best they can. You meet people just like them every day."

Kathy Fong Yoneda:

"The most successful fantasies are those in which the main character (usually the hero) has the personality quirks, traits, and feelings of the average person. They may be blessed (or cursed) with a certain particular talent or ability ('magic'), but they also carry the excess baggage of uncertainties, insecurities, and fears of past and present that haunt and shadow them, some of which the average person can closely identify and sympathize with — and for the average person viewing a Fantasy, it's the perfect way to confront those feelings vicariously — from the safety of their seats at the Cineplex or on the livingroom sofa at home!"

Two Exercises

Like other exercises I've suggested, the first one involves going to your favorite video store and checking out movies. I've used a few non-Fantasy characters to point out the similarities between them and Fantasy characters. Now you do the same. Go through your own library of videos or go to the video store and check out both Fantasy and other genre movies, some realistic, some not. See how the characters compare and if you find them archetypes or believable as someone you might know. If the hero spot is shared by more than one person (*Willow, The Lord of the Rings,* etc.), see which hero is the hero's hero, the reluctant hero, etc.

Pick a couple of the characters from the movies you've just seen and reverse their roles. Make little Willow into Madmartigan and vice versa. Change Frodo into Strider and Strider into Samwise. Play with the types and see what hybrids you come up with, and if any of them now fits into, or creates, a new category.

CHAPTER 5

BEASTIES, MAGIC BEINGS, AND FANTASTIC RACES

It may seem that a Fantasy story isn't Fantasy unless there is a beastie galloping through it. Not so. Neither *Big* nor *The Indian in the Cupboard* had strange beasties, nor did *Field of Dreams* and *Pirates of the Caribbean* unless you count ghosts. However, beasties, magical beings, and Fantastic Races do travel the highways and back roads of Fantasy regularly. Their functions vary, depending upon what they are.

Beasties

First let me say this: No matter how unfondly you look upon past blind dates, they do not qualify as "Beasties." They really do come under the umbrella term "human." Sorry about that.

The beastie categories break down this way:

1. Normal Beasties
    a. Good
    b. Bad
2. Unusual Beasties
    a. Native
        i. Good
        ii. Bad
    b. Non-native
        i. Good
        ii. Bad

Normal Beasties

Normal beasties are your standard dogs, cats, horses, cows, etc. They perform the usual animal duties such as pulling carts, carrying riders, and catching mice. The members of the Fellowship of the Ring ride normal horses and ponies and, at one point in the Shire, a normal-looking dog barks, in a normal manner, at a Ring Wraith.

Good Beasties

These are non-troublesome animals (other than the usual balking at a saddle or backing up when they should go forward) and are helpful to their masters in times of trouble (remember the mischievous ferrets in *The Beastmaster*)? Most normal beasties (especially the good ones), don't have magical powers, don't look very different from animals we already know, obey their masters, and provide companionship. They are rarely in the spotlight and their main function is to round out the background to provide as realistic a setting as possible. The following sets this up:

Example:
EXT. Middle European Village — Day
Market day, circa 1400. Pigs in pens, chickens in cages, and a few dogs run loose. A mule pulls a vegetable cart through the crowd. Two dragons appear in the sky, swoop down, and terrorize the people.

Your audience's subconscious processes this scene as familiar because it has seen it before in other non-Fantasy medieval movies such as *Robin Hood* or *Ivanhoe*. Everything is normal —

the people, the scene, the beasties — until the dragons show up and your audience realizes that it is not in history's Middle Europe anymore.

Bad Beasties
Can you say, *Cujo* or maybe *The Birds*? Normal beasties that are bad are bad for a variety of reasons.

1. They've been trained to be bad.
2. They're rabid, sick, or in pain.
3. They've been deliberately abused.
4. They're frightened.

Unlike the good beasties, the bad ones often take the spotlight and milk it for all it's worth. And why shouldn't they? They're supposed to scare the beegeebees out of the hero and the audience.

Bad beasties can be the usual domestics ones such as dogs, cats, cows, and chickens, or wild ones that pique our left over fears from the days when mankind wasn't at the top of the food chain: wolves (*Snow White*), snakes (*Indiana Jones*), sly things swimming in the water (*The Princess Bride*), and rats (*Indiana Jones*, again). Yup, there's nothing like a stalking animal to remind us that, given the right circumstances, we're just prey.

Normal Animals Gone Bad
Example: "Pretty Marianne walks through the woods. She doesn't notice as she kicks over a small mound in the grass. Angry ants swarm out of the mound and within moments...." Kinda makes your skin crawl, doesn't it?

Marianne's ants are normal in this scene, they're just reacting to having their home treated so rudely. Would you like it if someone kicked over yours?

But, what if Marianne doesn't kick over the mound and misses it completely? Why would these everyday ants swarm her if she were five feet away from the mound? Ants have an incredible sense of smell. What if they were trained to respond to a stimulus, perhaps Marianne's perfume? It could be sprayed near the mound and every time it is sprayed, the mound is destroyed. Then, when she does walk near it, the ants smell her perfume and decide to defend their home against this marauder.

Whether ants think like that or not is a matter of research (should you want to use the idea), but it certainly would turn a normal beastie into a bad one.

Unusual Beasties
Fortunately CGI now makes it easy to create many unusual animals. I don't know about you, but there's something rather laughable about a dog with big patches of fur attached all over it to make it look like a different animal. I've never been able to get beyond the prosthetics when they're used on animals.

Unusual beasties can be native, or not native, to the world you've created. The native creatures, no matter what they look like to the audience, perform all the same duties as real life animals. For example, instead of a horse, Luke Skywalker rides a Tauntaun on the planet Hoth in The Empire Strikes Back. Although no one in the film says, "The Tauntauns are native to this world," the audience accepts their presence as native.

A non-native beastie in a created world would be a surprise to its inhabitants, such as the flying imps in Ray Harryhausen's *The Golden Voyage of Sinbad*. In that movie you see the villain make one of the imps.

Good Unusual Beasties

The good beasties, like the Tauntauns, function the same as regular beasties. They pull plows, raise alarms and, although they look different than anything we know, provide the feeling that man and beast work together. These beasties exhibit all the same attributes we bestow on our own beasts: loyalty, affection, and protective instincts.

Bad Unusual Beasties

Again, these types of beasties can be normal to the world you created — such as the rodents of unusual size in *The Princess Bride* — or, they can be nasty pieces of work by the villain.

Unsure how to use the beasties and why? Here are four separate scenarios, all using a soft, fluffy white cat.

Fluffy's Excellent Adventures

Scenario #1, Fluffy as a good, normal beastie:
The evil wizard plots his best evil tricks while Fluffy purrs in his lap. This goes on several times during the script and it is a rather nice little touch. Here you have this nasty evildoer with a warm fuzzy in his lap. Anyone who likes a fluffy little animal can't be all bad, right? Maybe he can be talked into doing good instead of evil? Little Fluffy provides more than window-dressing, she shows a different side to the wizard.

Scenario #2, Fluffy as a bad normal beastie:
Fluffy sits in a wizard's lap, purring away. He feeds her a juicy little tidbit but she doesn't like the treat and chows down on his finger, instead. The wizard howls in rage and turns Fluffy into something really vile, or he sweeps her aside with such force that when she hits the wall she gives new meaning to the term "cata...PULT." This sequence shows that, despite having a nasty lap-pet, the evil wizard is just plain bad, too. Most real cat lovers (wizardly or not) would yelp, suck their fingers and then apologize to Fluffy for a) giving her a treat she didn't like or b) scaring her by screaming in agony.

Scenario #3, Fluffy as a good unusual beastie:
Fluffy sits in the sun washing her face. A dog walks by and she puffs up. You then see that every individual fur is a nasty, sharp quill. The dog leaves and the wizard's baby daughter crawls toward Fluffy. Fluffy immediately smoothes out her fur so a quill doesn't stick the baby. She's obviously unusual, but she is a sweetie to be so careful around the baby.

Scenario #4, Fluffy as a bad unusual beastie:
The hero threatens the evil wizard. As the hero advances on him, weapon upraised, the wizard flings Fluffy at him. While sailing through the air Fluffy's individual furs turn into poison-tipped quills and her big green eyes shoot black rays of death. She ceases, at this point, to be window dressing and is all hidden weapon. She's also a pet you don't want up on the bed at night.

Other Beastie Functions:
Beasties do more than fill in the background or create scary moments in films. They can provide comic relief or a five-hankie film.

Beasties as Comic Relief

From spitting camels to cats biting the wires of Christmas tree lights, beasties provide some of our favorite comic movie memories. So, having a Fantasy Beastie doing all the wacky and wonderful things our own pets do is both fine, and problematic. When using comic relief beasties, follow the same path you follow for comic relief characters, keep their moments brief and satisfying, and do not overuse them.

Example: Follow the comedy rule of three: establish, set-up, punch line. The first mishap establishes what the beastie does. This can be funny, or it can hint at possible funny moments in the future. The second mishap sets the stage for the punch line. The punch line can be used to thwart the enemy or get the hero into, or out of, danger. Sometimes it's fun for the audience to be able to spot the approaching punch line.

For instance: your beastie sneezes blue flame whenever he's around marigolds. The first time he sneezes he starts a bonfire, right where the hero sits. Result, singed hero and embarrassed beastie. The second time he sneezes is when the hero gives his lady love a bouquet with marigolds in it. That blue flame spooks her horse and the hero has to chase after her. The third time the Evil One has them surrounded at a cliff. But at the edge is a strip of marigolds. The audience will see what is coming and wait in anticipation for its natural outcome.

Beasties as comic relief can be a lot of fun, but when they're too cute, or seem to have no purpose other than comic relief, they can be too much. If you use them, use them well.

Beastie Tugging at Heart Strings

I don't know about you, but I can't watch a movie in which a pet gets killed without hauling out the tissues. I've been known to cry more about the trusty dog getting killed than the hero's demise.

Yes, you can use the death or the injury of a beastie — if you've written the critter so that it endears itself to the audience — to get the tissues flying. Some viewers might be annoyed because killing the animal is as much a cliché as the heroine twisting her ankle while running. Use this ploy with caution. It can backfire on you in a miserable way.

How do you create a beastie for your script? What kind of world have you created? Is it desert, forest, mountain, or marshland? The Worgs in *The Lord of the Rings* had a vague hyena-like look to them, plus they were in an area reminiscent of a savanna, where hyenas do live. You could say that the Worgs fit right into their surroundings. The same goes for the Wampa ice creature that attacked Luke Skywalker in *The Empire Strikes Back*. It fit in with its long fur and heavy body and was very believable. But, would you have believed a giant goldfish in all that snow?

If you want your beastie to be very unusual, maybe a "fish out of water," you should then create it to go against its surroundings. Be wild, be wacky, have a heck of a good time thinking up your beastie, but be logical and make sure there is a reason for it being in the story. If the hero has to battle a hairy-handed hog-swallower to get from Point A to Point A+, or to show his fallibility, or to prove his prowess with a sword and dirk, good. Put the beastie in the story and let rip. But don't put him in just because this is Fantasy. If the beastie is wasting script pages, it's wasting film time.

Magical Beings

Magical Beings are the creatures from myths and stories told 'round the campfire. Every culture has them, from the Banshees of the Irish to the Thunderbirds of Native North Americans. A partial listing would include: Unicorns, Griffons, Harpies, Pegasus, Djin, Dragons, and the Hydra.

Dragons are probably the most popular magical beings, since they appear in various myths and stories the world over. The dragons of Middle Europe are usually greedy, not very nice, and have a virgin fetish, however, they can be good, too, depending on the tale being told. They're the villains in *Dragonslayer* and the good guy in *Dragonheart*. The European dragons are like flying reptiles with scales and flesh-ripping claws. The dragons of the Orient are considered to be good and represent the Earth elements. They're very different looking than the European dragon and are sometimes made up of different creatures' parts such as camels and deer.

Unicorns are the next favorite among the beings. Their single, spiral horns are supposed to hold great magic and power. For this reason, they are hunted, much like ivory poachers hunt elephants for their tusks. The best way to catch a unicorn is to use a virgin as bait.

Djin, or Genies are also very popular. I've seen people in antique shops pick up an old Aladdin-style oil lamp, glance around and, when they think no one is looking, give the lamp a rub. There are different types of djin and they're not always stuck in lamps for thousands of years — they do attach to other personal items such as jewelry. Some djin are nice, some are naughty, and some are downright nasty. Djin can be considered both magical beings and/or a fantastic race.

Don't limit yourself, should you want to include a magical being in your script, to the ones that are well known. Do a little research and find one that's just right for your story, or make your own. A book you might want to look through for more in-depth information (and anecdotes with people who claim to have seen some of these beings) is Cassandra Eason's *A Complete Guide to Faeries & Magical Beings: Explore the Mystical Realm of the Little People.*

As with beasties, there should be a logical reason to have a magical being in your script. It could be simple: A griffon draws a wizard's cart. Or it could be complicated: A legion of djin fight in the battle of good versus evil. The beings can also be window dressing: A school for wizards has a riding stable of unicorns and winged horses.

No matter how big a part magical beings play in your script, their presence should feel natural and right to the audience.

Fantastic Races

Fantastic Races should not be confused with magical beings or beasties. But how can you tell the difference between a race and a magical being? "Race" in the dictionary is denoted as a large group of people, animals, or plants with similar characteristics, i.e. you can have a race of fish or plants. Another definition includes common traits and a unifying culture. Obviously, this is a subject that could spawn a book or two of its own, but for my book, members of a "race" are humanoid.

Elves are thought to have pointed ears. The Lord of the Rings: The Two Towers *(2002)*

So, with the humanoid criteria, what can be considered a Fantastic Race for Fantasy? Elves, Dwarves, Giants, Leprechauns, Merpeople, Centaurs, Fairies, Nymphs, Trolls, and Djin to name a few. These races are known in many cultures, with fairies and elves being top favorites.

Common characteristics associated with the individual races are: Elves have pointy ears and live in the forest. Dwarves are short, stocky, bearded, and live in caves or under the mountains. Giants are huge, usually not very bright and sometimes, fe-fi-fo-fum, eat humans. Leprechauns are teensy, little people who live in Ireland and have a pot of gold hidden somewhere. Merpeople, of course, have fish tails instead of legs, live in the oceans and, depending on which legend you're reading, either lure sailors to their doom, or fall in love with them and want to be human. Centaurs are savage, heavy drinkers, their blood is poisonous, and the males like human women. Fairies are usually thought of as small, with wings, although some are full human sized and they can fool humans with illusions. They also like to mess around in human affairs. Nymphs are usually beautiful women and are associated with trees, rivers, and streams. There are also lake and sea nymphs, not to be confused with merpeople. Trolls, traditionally, are big but not as big as giants, intelligent, and live under bridges and in mountain caves.

There are many other fantastic races such as Cyclopes, Goblins, Sprites, Gnomes, Pixies, and Satyrs. But why, if you're writing a Fantasy, do you have to stick with the established races? Swift created the Houyhnhnms in *Gulliver's Travels*, Tolkien wrote about the Hobbits and Ents, Robert Jordan in *The Wheel of Time* series gave us the Aiel, and George Lucas created Wookies and Ewoks for the *Star War* movies. If you want to create a new race, by all means do! After all, there is absolutely nothing to stop you.

If this new race you develop is an important part of your story, make sure the audience can identify its people by having one or two individuals, with multi-dimensional personalities, represent it. Chewbacca shows that Wookies are strong and independent. They're also good friends and intelligent. If he were nothing more than a lumbering giant in the background, he would only be window dressing in the movie. Instead he's a whole character, right down to his sense of humor.

As I said in the beginning of this chapter, you don't have to have a beastie, magical being, or fantastic race in your story. It can still be a wonderful story without them. But, if you feel that you should, research the well-known ones and either choose one, or make up your own. You can even use an amalgam of different beings, a little like a mixed-breed dog that turns out to have the best traits of each breed, or maybe, the worst.

An Exercise

Pick an unusual beastie (not anything like a dog or horse) from one of your favorite movies, it doesn't matter what it is. Now list everything you can remember about it — size, looks, how it walks, if it talks, or just makes noise, etc. Now compare it to animals (it doesn't matter which animals) in our real world. How different is it? How alike is it? Is it made up of several different types of animals?

Fix a real animal (cat, dog, aardvark) in your mind and build on it to create an unusual beastie. Try NOT to use any of the actual parts from a real animal like lop-ears, webbed toes, etc.

CHAPTER 6

MAGIC

On the Subject of Magic:

"Magic is science that hasn't been proven."

— Unknown.

Magic. It's a fascinating subject. So fascinating that hundreds of books have been written about it and, as I mentioned in Chapter Two, people have devoted their lives to its study. Not the magic of flashy Las Vegas magicians, but the Earth magic of village wise women, wizards, witches, shamans, and more. All the information available can't be covered in one small chapter, nor does it need to be. This is a book about screenwriting. Vast amounts of background knowledge about magic's history and practice through the centuries isn't something you must have (although it wouldn't hurt). What I'll try to do in this chapter is provide insights into magic and its use within the confines of a script. I strongly suggest further research.

The practice of magic goes back thousands of years, with written records first showing up in the time of the ancient Egyptians. Throughout these thousands of years (and probably back to primitive man), magic has meant different things to different people, just like today. For some people all magic is evil and the work of the devil. To others, it's a way of life, on a daily basis. Our cultures dictate our views of magic. For instance:

An adventurer wanders into a primitive village, fires a gun, kills the local chief and, because of his "death stick," is proclaimed a great sorcerer. (Lord, help him when he runs out of ammo.) Now take the same man and let him loose in a modern North Woods township in the United States. When he shoots the local mayor he'll learn what "open season" really means. In one culture the adventurer is a fearsome sorcerer, in the other he's nothing but a common thug.

Because movies wield such a strong influence with modern man, it shouldn't be a surprise that opinions of magic are formed on what he sees in the theater and on TV. To many people, magic is meals popping up out of nowhere, blue balls of flame tossed back and forth between wizards, and people turned into, as Samwise Gamgee puts it, something "unnatural."

Is what you know about magic based on what you've seen in the movies and on TV? Here's a little test. Make a list of 10 things you think you know about magic. Now go over your list and, next to every item, write down where you learned your information. If your biggest influence has been the movies or TV, you need to expand your view of magic. You can make your script unique and desirable if you utilize new uses of the craft. But how do you expand your view? How else, but with research?

There are so many rites, rituals, and customs that exist in this world — and have never been seen in a movie — it's a shame to ignore them. Not all of them are magical, but with a little ingenuity, they could be and therefore perfectly usable in your script.

I love this old Scottish custom that I found in a slim, little book titled *Scottish Customs* by Sheila Livingstone: Two nuts, one representing a woman, the other a man, are placed in a fire. If the nuts burn quietly side-by-side the couple's union will do well, but if the nuts burst, their love will be troublesome. An old wive's tale, right? It could be, but how about if your script's first scene shows John and Jane celebrating their engagement with family and friends? Along comes old Auntie Maude with two walnuts. She places them in the fireplace while people laugh at her. After all, this is a silly old custom and everyone knows that John and Jane are made for each other. A crack and a pop and all eyes turn to the fire in horror. One of the nuts has split open, its raw edges blackened by the fire. Can you say, "foreshadowing?" It's not magic, *per se*, but it is something on which you can build a story. *Scottish Customs* is not a book of magic, but of customs and superstitions that go back long before Christianity came to Scotland. You'll find many books written on the subject of different customs from different countries. They're not only interesting, but definitely worth a look.

Below are some questions that are based on old wives' tales, true happenings, and maybe a few magical connections. How many of them can you answer?

1. What is a Rusalka?
2. What does red thread do?
3. What is the basic power of Vanilla?

4. What are the four elements?

5. What are the associated deities of the herb Mugwort?

6. Why is carrying a spade on your shoulder through a house considered unlucky?

7. What powers does the Rowan tree have?

8. If a household pet sneezes near a bride on her wedding day what will happen?

9. What is the Specter of Broken?

10. What was special about the Witch of Newbury, England?

Here are the answers:

1. A Rusalka, in Slavic folklore, is a spirit or water nymph. Her soul is that of a young woman or girl who died a violent death. The spirits of these hapless girls inhabit lakes and try to lure young men to their deaths. A Rusalka's fate can be undone by avenging her death.

2. Red thread that is knotted is a charm against the evil eye.

3. Vanilla's basic power is love.

4. The four elements are Air, Earth, Fire, and Water.

5. Mugwort's associated deities are Artemis and Diana.

6. Carrying a spade across your shoulder in the house means a grave will be dug soon.

7. The Rowan tree has the powers of healing and protection.

8. If a household pet sneezes near a bride on her wedding day she will have good luck in her marriage.

9. The Specter of Broken is a natural light phenomenon. When someone stands on a mountain peak, the light shining behind him that bounces off clouds or fog will result in a shadow resembling an elongated man with

rays of light coming from his head and hands. On occasion you'll find a photo of this on the Web. Of the six or seven photos I've seen, the Specter is quite eerie and could lend itself well to a Fantasy. (one picture is at: *http://www.terragalleria.com/mountain/mountain-image.alps3015.html*) The phenomenon is named after Mount Broken in the Harz mountain range in northern Germany, a rumored favorite spot of witches.

10. The Witch of Newbury was a surfer babe. Soldiers of the Earl of Essex found a woman riding a wooden plank across the waves in the river. Convinced she was a witch, they ambushed and killed her when she came ashore. There's also another story about another woman seen walking on the water (it's thought she was on stilts) in 1643. Soldiers shot at her, but she — supposedly — laughed as she caught their bullets and then chewed upon them. That is, until one found its mark. It appears that women with unusual abilities during that time period were very suspect.

I found these interesting tidbits by opening two folklore books at random pages, and one quick look on the Web. Obviously it doesn't take much to expand a person's view of magic, legend, and myth! There is a world of wild and wonderful information waiting to be explored and used by you.

Now that I've (hopefully) impressed upon you the fact that you don't have to drive yourself nuts creating new and improved magic for your script, you need to ask yourself another question:

What Purpose Does Magic Have in Your Script?

Magic is expected in a Fantasy, but if it doesn't have a purpose, it won't work for the audience. In *Practical Magic* Sally Owens claims she doesn't want to have anything to do with magic. As much as she has a natural talent for it (remember she comes from a long line of witches), she ignores it. Or does she? She lights candles by blowing on them and her coffee stirrers continue to stir after she's let them go. These brief moments are shown every time she claims she doesn't want to have anything to do with magic. They tell the audience, very clearly, that she's not being honest with herself. In addition, her actions create an important set up for the end of the movie when she finally embraces her talent.

Magic has its limits in The Lord of the Rings: The Two Towers *(2002)*

I ask again: What purpose does magic have in your script? Does it start the story off, i.e., John jogs down the street, steps in a fairy ring and POOF! He's gone! Or, does magic further the plot, i.e., Gandalf speaking to a moth at the top of Saruman's tower? Does it save or ruin the day? Is it important to your story, or is it there "just because?"

If you say magic is in your script "just because," you're in deep doo-doo. In every Fantasy, magic has to have a purpose. Wait. I take that back... in every GOOD Fantasy, magic has to have a purpose. The magic in the *Harry Potter* stories does. It helps solve mysteries, destroy evil, protect Harry and his friends, and helps him grow as a person. In *The Lord of the Rings*, magic destroys demons, saves heroes and, without the magic ring of power, there is no story.

If you're not sure what purpose magic serves in your script — other than lots of fun effects — determine what sub-genre you're writing. Is it a romance, or maybe a coming-of-age movie? In a romance, the magic can have different effects. It can bring the lovers together, then separate them and then bring them together again (*Practical Magic*). Or, it can separate them and they have to find a way to overcome it (*Ladyhawke*). In a coming of age film like *The Indian in the Cupboard*, magic gives Omri his first steps toward growing up, and the magic in *The Neverending Story* convinces Bastian that he's not insignificant. As you can see, magic is only one of the components in a Fantasy story.

Some writers attempting their first Fantasy scripts may look upon magic as the perfect chance to provide the production company with page after page of fabulous effects, each one better than the one before. Sorry, but that's been done, over and over and over again. Which is why we keep seeing that same old blue ball of flame tossed from wizard to wizard through movie to movie. All we need is a split screen and a game of "Pass it on." As I said earlier in this chapter, there is a wealth of magical customs, rites, and rituals that have never been seen in a movie. You can make your script stand out by using them.

With so much written about magic, it's almost easier to research than the legends of the Bible. Most libraries and bookstores have occult sections and many towns and cities have either New Age or occult stores where you can find books on magic. If you don't feel comfortable walking into an occult book store (some people don't, there's no shame in it) talk to your local librarian and tell her what you're researching and why. She should be able to point you in the right direction. I'll put another plug in for my favorite type of books here... the encyclopedias. They'll help you wade through tons of information so you can pull out what you need and focus your search in the correct areas.

Unless you know specifically what you're looking for, I don't advise turning to the Web for your first foray into the subject. As good as it is, we all know how much misinformation is on the Web, so it behooves you to start out with a solid footing. I've surfed around quite a bit while researching this book and frankly, there are some Web sites out there that can best be described as: "Wow, woo-woo-land." Magic is very logical and has a long history. Some of these sites defied logic. Look through more established and respected works on the subject before you turn to the Web.

The practice of magic, as I said earlier, is thousands of years old. Records of its use are found all over the world and, with such a background, you can bet there is a lot of conflicting information available. So how do you decide what to use and what not to use in a script?

Let logic be your guide. No matter where magic was practiced there were always basic laws that had to be followed so it would work properly. Have your characters follow rules, unless, of course, you WANT things to go wrong to further the story. Also, match the magic to your setting. If an Aztec-style blood rite seems out of place in your script, don't use it. If it strikes *you* as out of place, it will be out of place to everyone else reading the script.

Ever wonder where all that stuff comes from when a witch or wizard conjures it up out of mid-air? There are a few theories on it. Exploration of that question can provide interesting twists to your script.

In a fun little movie called *Bernard and the Genie*, Bernard (Alan Cumming) rubs a magic lamp and finds himself saddled with an exuberant Genie (Lenny Henry). After an initial show of power, the Genie confesses he's delighted to be released from his lamp after 2000 years and will grant Bernard's wishes. Bernard is an art dealer, so he wishes that the Mona Lisa was hanging on his wall. The Genie obliges and Bernard sits back to enjoy Mona's smile. Of course, in order for the Genie to give Mona to Bernard, she has to go missing from the Louvre. Magic often marches to the beat of: For every action there is a reaction.

In *The Lord of the Rings: The Two Towers* there is a brilliant sequence in which Gandalf casts Saruman from his possession of King Theodan of Rohan. When Gandalf whacks Theodan with his staff, the film cuts directly to Saruman as he is flung across the hall of Isengard. Again an excellent example of action = reaction. Of course you don't HAVE to show this in your script every time you use magic — people tend to accept wizards conjuring things out of nothing, but using the "action = reaction" theory you can add extra depth to your story. Plus it's a great device in a comedy.

Types of Magic
There are many, many ways to practice magic. Here are but a few:

Spells and Curses. Surprisingly enough, most of us utter spells and incantations on a daily basis. Prayers are a form of spell. I have a friend who is notorious for losing things and finding them again, quickly. She innocently told me one day that when she loses something she simply "repeats a spell of finding" and the lost items shows up within a day or two. Not unlike losing your keys when you're late for work and repeating over and over "Please let me find my keys, please, please, please."

Potions. Potions are recipes that do all sorts of wonderful and/or nasty things, from the famous "Love Potion #9" to the poison contained in Snow White's apple. Usually, potions are concocted while a spell is being repeated over them. They're made from a variety of herbs and, sometimes, nasty things like eye of newt and wart of toad. (By the way, some newts are highly toxic, which is why you usually hear of their body parts being used in evil spells.)

Divination. Ah yes, foretelling the future. From reading runes to consulting the stars or the entrails of a goat killed at 4:45 in the morning under a waning moon, the magician is supposed to be able to tell what the future holds. He doesn't always do that, however, and that can change a story considerably, if his foretelling skills are lacking. You can find a glossary of divination techniques at: *http://www.angelfire.com/tx/afaceinacrowd/gloss-div.html*

Scrying. Scrying is a technique of divination usually limited to gazing into a crystal ball or a mirror (Frodo did it in Galadrial's water basin that she called a mirror).

Rituals and rites. These are ceremonies and services following specific rules and activities. Quite often, you'll see them used in the movies for Black Magic purposes, surrounded by dancing girls, beating drums, and some poor person writhing on an alter of stone.

Astrology. Another way of telling the future. There are forms of astrology everywhere in the world, from the Egyptians to the Aztecs.

The people in your script who handle magic can use any, or all, of these types, and the many others that exist. Some practitioners are better at one than another. You'll want to take this into account when deciding what type of magic your character handles and how it will play into your story. If it doesn't matter, then you needn't worry about it. But giving each magic person in your script a specialty can add more depth.

Magic's Limitations

Too often I hear non-Fantasy fans say something like, "Why doesn't the magician just wave his wand and get the characters out of the mess they're in?" My response is, "Then there wouldn't be a story." This answer usually satisfies them but the truth is, magic is not an absolute. Not only does it have limits, it needs them.

The Lord of the Rings: The Fellowship of the Ring has a great sequence in the mines of Moria when Gandalf lets his fellow travelers know that what they face (the Balrog) is something they can't fight. The best thing they can do is run for their lives. When they reach a strategic bridge he uses his magic to collapse it under the Balrog. He knows his magic is not strong enough to fight the Balrog, but it is strong enough to collapse the bridge, which will cause the Balrog to fall to its death.

Gandalf's power and rank are denoted by the color of his clothing. Saruman is Saruman the White and Gandalf is Gandalf the Grey. Although it is not stated in the film that a White Wizard has more power than a Grey, it is evident when Gandalf cannot win his first fight against Saruman. In order for Gandalf to expand his power, he dies and is brought back, stronger. When he comes back he is Gandalf the White and the audience knows immediately that he is now on equal footing with Saruman.

Your story can have many reasons why the magic in it has limits:

1. The practitioner's skill/power level. Some are stronger, and better at making magic than others. How else would one magician win in a fight with another?

2. The tools used are defective, of poor quality, dirty, or even cursed. Whatever the reason, the tool being used in a magical rite is not proper and this will limit the magic being wrought.

3. The magic being wrought is being done incorrectly. It's like using soda water instead of baking soda in a cake recipe; it just won't work (don't laugh, I know someone who did that).

4. The timing is off. That may sound silly, but many magic rites often must take place at a specific time of day or during a lunar cycle. If you perform the rite at another time it won't work or... the results can be pretty darned awful.

5. The practitioner is not committed to what he is doing. It doesn't work when a magician calls in his performance.

There are many more reasons why magic is limited and you, as the writer, can have as much fun thinking up reasons to limit it, as to use it.

Magic Is Neutral

You're probably wondering why I haven't brought up the subject of Black Magic. Well, that's because magic is like karma, it is directly affected by the person wielding it. If he has evil intentions you've got evil (black) magic. If his intentions are good, you've got good (white) magic. This interpretation has been debated through the centuries and will continue to be debated for many more. It all depends on whom you talk to. Many mainstream religions believe that ALL magic is bad. Some Black Magic rites would make you shudder. However, you'll discover that those rites actually were based on "holy" rites channeled toward a darker purpose by the practitioner.

Black Magic, as seen in movies and on TV usually involves a blood sacrifice (often children), demons, Satan and, quite often, sex. If anything goes against the mores of an established society, you can bet it will find itself included in a Black Magic rite. The first recorded Black Mass (there are conflicting opinions on this) was in 1673 at the request of, believe it or not, the mistress of Louis XIV, Madame de Montespan. She felt she had fallen out of favor with him and the mass was held to make him love her. When it failed, she tried another Black Mass to bring about his death. (Note: Don't confuse the first recorded date of the Black Mass with Black Magic in general.)

It's reasonable to assume that if a character in a movie is practicing a form of Black Magic, he or she is the villain. He doesn't have to be. He could be someone who has been lead astray and your hero is out to save him. Or he could be misguided. Or, in classic happy-ending style, he could see the error of his ways and come over to the good side. The choice is yours.

Magic for Personal Gain

Burn this into your brain: The good guy doesn't use magic for personal gain except to introduce conflict into your story. Think (I know, I ask you to do that a lot) about all the stories, books, movies, and TV shows you've seen in which magic is used for personal gain. Who uses it that way? The bad guy, right? If the good guy does that he ends up regretting it.

Gandalf turns down the ring because he knows that, even though he would try to use it for good, he wouldn't. When *does* he use his magic? To save people and cast out demons. Bernard finds out the hard way about using magic for personal gain when the police arrest him for stealing the Mona Lisa. Sally Owens, in her grief, begs her aunts to bring back her dead husband. They inform her that if they did that, it wouldn't be him but something loathsome and terrible. Although Harry Potter's friends could be considered poor, they don't use magic for personal gain, and those who do in the stories, find out why they shouldn't.

Yes, your magic-wielding characters can use their skills to light lamps (a personal gain in the fact that they won't stumble around in the dark now), stir coffee, glue a ripped hem, or clean house quickly. In these instances magic is nothing but a tool, much like a computer is a tool for a writer. True personal gain would be amassing riches, putting spells on people to love you against their will, or attaining ultimate power over others.

If you tempt your good characters into using magic for personal gain, you immediately introduce a new avenue of conflict in your story: Remember the moment of "oh no" when Samwise held the Ring of Power in his hands? Conflict is good as it moves your story along. However, if your good character uses magic for personal gain as a matter of course, this is not good. That's the bad guy's job.

Tools of the Trade

In the TV mini-series *Merlin*, Sam Neill (as Merlin) describes himself as a "hand magician." In other words, he has to use his hands in order to make his magic work. He can't use a wand or staff or even a twig, he has to use his hands. This could present problems if his hands are tied behind his back.

There are standard tools of the trade in the magic business.

1. The wand.
2. Candles.
3. The staff.
4. The cauldron.
5. Herbs.
6. A mortar and pestle to grind the herbs.
7. Bones.
8. Runes.
9. Ashes.
10. Animal parts — what can I say — a little eye of newt.
11. Incense.
12. Non-sacrificial animals, i.e., familiars.

The list of tools is as endless and as limitless as your imagination. Who says a magician can't use a Mont Blanc pen instead of a wand? Or a witch can't scry from her Esté Lauder compact instead of a broken mirror from Great-Great-Auntie Isadorra? And just exactly who said that you HAVE to use a magic mirror if you really want to use a shiny, new hubcap? I repeat, the list of the tools of the trade is as endless as your imagination. Fit the right tool to the personality of your character. If I could wield a magic wand it would probably be my very "girlie" ballpoint pen with the lilacs printed all over it. What would your wand be?

Tools aren't always a must for your magic person. Samantha of *Bewitched* fame wiggled her nose, while her cousin, Sabrina waved her arms like a landing albatross and Sam's mother merely snapped her fingers or waved her hand.

Animals have long been thought of as having certain powers. Frogs and elephants are considered good luck. Bears have healing powers. Bulls are associated with a variety of religions and are often the symbol of strength or fertility. The swan is the symbol of the muses and Native Americans look upon the coyote as a trickster. When searching for a tool or symbol for your magic person, or anyone else in your story, don't forget animals. Many magicians keep animals to help guide them in visions or to act as shields against spells and curses directed their way.

Who Handles Magic?

Anyone. Anyone in a script can handle magic; it depends on you, the author, to decide whom you want handling it. But, there are the stereotypical users.

1. Witches and Sorceresses.
2. Wizards and Sorcerers.
3. Magical Beings.
4. Magical Races.
5. Commoners with talent.

There is no set rule that says only a select few can handle magic. I have not seen, nor read, a story in which everyone handles it (not everyone in a *Harry Potter* story handles magic), but when everyone has magic abilities the story boils down to who's the strongest or the cleverest, who uses it wisely, and who uses it foolishly.

Who Shouldn't Handle Magic?

This is the fun part of Fantasy writing. The obvious, logical, answer is: The Bad Guy. After all, it gives him an edge over everyone else, it makes him (supposedly) invincible, it lets him do dastardly things and it is often the driving force behind the movie, i.e., stop the creep before he takes over the world and enslaves everyone else to do his evil biddings. Like I said, lots of fun.

The other person who shouldn't, logically, handle magic is the ditz. You know the character, no sense, common or otherwise, a total clutz, always in trouble, like Mickey in *The Sorcerer's Apprentice*, adorable but definitely not capable. Magic, in the hands of the inept, is as dangerous as it is in the hands of a knowledgeable Bad Guy. Fortunately, the inept usually gains control of his powers at a crucial moment in the movie and saves the day. It doesn't have to be this way, however. There can be added interest if the inept can't figure out just how he managed to pull it together and the movie ends with him still having difficulty. (This also allows for the possibility of a sequel.)

Want to stir up a heap of trouble in a story? Give the magic to a spurned woman. Or give it to a dog so that something happens when he barks and it takes the hero forever to find out just why his sword keeps turning into a flamingo at the wrong time.

When you give magic to the person who shouldn't have it, make sure you don't limit yourself to the usual people. Remember addled Aunt Clara on *Bewitched*? Magic in her hands provided some of the funniest episodes of the series. And, of course, magic in the hands of the baby Tabitha, before she understood the responsibility that came with her power, was always good for a laugh.

Which gives you another person who shouldn't wield magic. The person with no sense of the responsibility he now holds. Again, by giving this person power, you can open up all kinds of interesting avenues for your story. So go for it, give it to someone who shouldn't, logically, have it and see what happens.

What They Say & an Exercise, All in One!

C.S. Friedman: Author of *The Coldfire Trilogy*, and *In Conquest Born*, among other novels. Ms. Friedman is also a guest lecturer in both writing and costume. (*http://www.csfriedman.com*)

C. S. Friedman's "Dungeonmaster Rule" for the creation of realistic magic systems:
"Any story with magic in it must have inherent in the very nature of that magic, some feature that limits its use."

Explanation:
It's easy to get so lost in a story concept that you forget to ask yourself what "real" people would do with your magic, i.e., characters who don't have a vested interest in seeing your plot go where you want it to go. Sometimes it's hard, as an author, to step back and get that perspective. So, as an exercise, envision a group of Fantasy game players, with nothing better to do than search for loopholes in our creation that they can exploit for personal gain. As the Dungeonmaster, your job is to design a world in which that exploitation will be kept to a minimum — or at least to within limits that won't overwhelm or derail your story — without having to bring in characters who will tell them not to do things.

Not only will this make the world more realistic, but it may actually give rise to interesting new ideas and add to the world-creation process.

Example:
Is there any point at which a wizard in your story conjures an item out of thin air? It doesn't matter if it's a magical scroll or a speck of dust. As soon as you establish that mass can be created out of nothing, the savvy player will ask why he can't just conjure a palace full of gold and hire other people to do all his adventuring for him.

So, perhaps you decide there is a limit to how much mass can be conjured at one time. The savvy player responds "make it diamonds, then," and goes on with his plan as before. Perhaps you, then, add that the mass doesn't "actually" come out of nowhere, in fact there is an expenditure of some nonmaterial force, or a transfer from another dimension required... whatever it is, expect the player's next fixation to be on how he will obtain more of this "fuel" than you ever intended a character to have.

Or, perhaps the mass only holds its new form temporarily? Expect, then, that the players will design vast con jobs which entail paying for services and goods in ways that guarantee their characters are long gone when the payment ceases to exist. A palace full of "temporary" gold is fine if you are not in town when it dissolves....

Now, you may note that the last two additions can lead to interesting story possibilities in their own right. Perverse though it may sound, the process of putting limits upon "magic" can often inspire great story lines.

CHAPTER 7

LOCATION

Why Central Europe?

Movie viewers around the world think of Fantasy within the confines of their own locales and cultures. Many of Bollywood's first movies concerned the myths and legends of India's rich culture. The Far Eastern films — including Japanese animation — also reflect thousands of years of culture. It's not surprising then, that Western Culture people think of Fantasy as taking place in lands that resemble medieval Central Europe.

As a writer of Fantasy you owe it to yourself to explore the many different cultures of our Earth. Here are but a few areas other than Central Europe.

1. South America.
2. Egypt.
3. The WHOLE continent of Africa.
4. Polynesia.
5. Easter Island.
6. Australia and New Zealand. (New Zealand has already established itself as a great place to film Fantasy.)
7. North America and its many native people.
8. China.

It's easy to see, when looking into the different myths and legends around the world that the existence of a "collective memory" is, in my opinion, a reality and not just a theory. Winged serpents, sea monsters, humans pitted against the Gods, Priests with magical powers, wise women, scryers, sages, mages, children born with "the sight," and, of course, the coming of "The One" are everywhere. It would be criminal to ignore these offerings.

Fantasy stories don't have to take place in strange countries or realms. The Indian in the Cupboard *(1995)*

Of course, "Location" doesn't have to be a continent or an island or a landlocked country. You can place your story in any geographical or geological spot.

1. On or inside a mountain.
2. On or under water such as an ocean, a lake, a pond, a river, or a puddle.
3. A desert.

4. A swamp.

5. A marsh.

6. A prairie.

7. On a tree's branches or inside a tree.

8. In the clouds.

9. In a person's mind.

10. In outer space.

Remember Tim Burton's *The Nightmare Before Christmas*? This delightful Fantasy's worlds were traveled to through various holiday trees. And what about *Alice In Wonderland's* world? She fell down a rabbit hole to get there. Dorothy in *The Wizard of Oz* went to a strange land that still felt very familiar to the audience. It had a look of a child's illustrated book, but very definitely American, with Middle European overtones. You're dealing with Fantasy, create the world that works best for your story.

An Exercise

Make a list of all the places in the world that you would like to visit or have already visited. What makes them special to you? How different are the cultures from your own? If you wrote a Fantasy set in one of these places, how would it differ from one set in medieval Europe? Pick two of the places that you'd like to visit, and one unique place, like inside a mountain or down a rabbit hole. Now create a thumbnail sketch of a Fantasy story you'd like to do and place it in each one of the three places. How does the location affect, or not affect, the story and the characters? Which one of the locations do you think you'd enjoy writing about the most?

CHAPTER 8

BATTLES
WITHIN AND WITHOUT

People who don't like Fantasy films sometimes complain that: "It's just one big battle after another." Of course they express this view after seeing an epic or adventure Fantasy such as *The Mummy* or *The Lord of the Rings*. My patience wears thin with these people and it's all I can do not to say: "Well, DUH? What did you expect? Didn't you see the trailers?" These movies were made to attract a younger, male crowd (although *The Lord of the Rings* has a much larger fan base) and that particular demographic *prefers* limb lopping and guts and gore.

To those of you who claim that Fantasy stories are nothing but big battles with death, doom, and destruction, step up to the plate, I have a few curve balls I'd like to slip past you:

1. *It's a Wonderful Life*
2. *Big*
3. *Field of Dreams*
4. *The Indian in the Cupboard*

Please describe, in 100 words or less, where the big, bloody battles are in these movies? The reason you can't do it is because these films have inner battles in which the protagonist has to learn something very important about himself and his relationship with the world.

"But," you ask, "why use Fantasy to tell a tale of self-discovery? Why not write a drama?" My answer is, "Sometimes, the only way reality happens is if there's a little magic flitting through a life." Let's face it, for many of us a life-changing epiphany (maybe even a miracle) is the closest we'll ever get to real magic, so why NOT make your story a Fantasy?

Movies with Big Bloody Battles

Not all battles have to be bloody. No, I'm not repeating myself, I mean it, literally. You don't have to have running rivulets of red blood in the sand — especially if a movie wants to keep a PG-13 rating. *The Mummy* and *The Mummy Returns* have terrific, edge-of-your-seat battles, but very little blood. Both movies also have some creep-you-out-down-to-your-toes moments, but they were great fun at the same time.

How do you write battle scenes (with or without buckets of blood)? Every scripting book or guru tells a writer to keep descriptions to a minimum. You're writing the script not directing the movie, so only put in what you need. It's sound advice. But how do you avoid the Goldilocks dilemma, i.e., What's too little, too much and just right? Here's the same scene, written three ways.

1. Ext. Battlefield — Night
Ten thousand mounted knights ride down upon the hordes of hell.

2. Ext. Battlefield — Night
By the light of the full moon, 10,000 mounted knights ride down upon the hordes of hell as they dance around bonfires. Beasts scream, hoof beats thunder, swords scrape on shields.

3. Ext. Battlefield — Night
A cloud skitters across the full moon. For a moment all is silent.
Ten thousand knights, their livery creaking in the damp night air,
move forward in the darkness from the top of the hill. In the val-
ley below, the hordes of hell dance around towering bonfires. A
beast screams in the moonlight, and thundering hoof beats grow
louder and louder. The riders burst forward. First one knight, then
another and another pull swords from scabbards. The sound of
steel raking across shields adds to the terror they bring.

Example #1 has plenty of information. With the rest of the
script to draw on, the director and set designer will know what
to do with what is there. However, Example #2 is better because
it offers more information (there's a full moon) and thus a clear-
er picture, plus if the hordes dancing around bonfires haven't
been mentioned before — but are important — now is the time
to introduce them. The last sentence, "Beasts scream, hoof
beats thunder, swords scrape on shields," could be left out,
however, its staccato beat creates a mood and introduces
sound. It is a personal call on whether to include it or not. Both
Example #1 and #2 assume that the comment "ride down
upon" gives the reader and director the idea that the knights are
on a hill overlooking the battlefield. The choice is yours whether
to state this in the description or not. Example #3 is okay, if
you're writing a book, and even then it should be refined.

This scene (using Example #2) works for introducing the battle,
but that's it. From there you should move to individual
moments within the battle, interspersed with sporadic
overviews. Something like:

Series of shots:
1. Jamie severs the hand of the Evil One's minion. The hand runs away into the thick of the battle.
2. Cassandra ducks when a Bulock swings his mace at her. The mace sails by and imbeds itself into the Bulock fighting with Jamie.
3. A sweeping view of the battle as the battalion forms a pincer maneuver.
4. Jamie and Cassandra stand back to back as they fight off glowing green imps.

You need not spend a full page describing how the green blood of the Evil One's minion spurts in a long arch with every beat of his unnatural evil heart until, in the throes of agony, he falls to his knees, screaming curses to the skies, etc., etc., etc., and etc. The director, prop guy, set designer, cameraman, and anyone else involved in the scene will provide the extra action needed... as will the actors.

If, within the battle, there are specific short shots that need to be included to further the story, then you bounce back and forth between them in a montage.

Montage:
1: Jamie runs into the castle.
2: Cassandra battles the Evil Sorcerer's apprentice.
3: Jamie searches for the fair Elaine.
4: Cassandra loses her sword to the apprentice and pulls out her dirk.
5: Jamie and Elaine escape the castle.
6: Cassandra, bloody dirk in hand, joins Jamie and Elaine.

Scenes from the bigger battle, concerning other characters, can also be interspersed between these six scenes. However, if you want these scenes to include more information and some dialogue, it's best to individualize them.

In a spec script you'll want to follow the general rules of format. If you're working on an assignment with a producer and a director, you'll have more leeway in how you format your script, how much description you add, etc.

As most huge battles are viewed fleetingly in a series of shots or montages, CGI images help save on the budget and "a cast of thousands" is no longer needed. However, the important scenes are the scenes in which the hero and the supporting characters are fighting one-to-one with the enemy and are shot close up.

Sometimes the inner battles of the characters are more devastating than the physical battles. The Lord of the Rings: The Fellowship of the Ring *(2001)*

Are Big Battles Necessary?

In some stories, yes. All of the battles in *The Lord of the Rings* films (even the cartoon versions) are necessary because this is a tale about the ultimate fight between good and evil. That's going to take more men than a small skirmish patrol. Here is where CGI is a blessing to filmmakers. Peter Jackson and his crew produced exceptional battle scenes and I particularly liked his nod to Leni Riefenstahl's propaganda films in the awe-inspiring gathering of Saruman's troops.

Kenneth Branagh's non-Fantasy film of Shakespeare's *Henry V* is an excellent movie to watch to get a feel for how to create big battle scenes with a limited cast and limited budget. Branagh focused totally on the men involved in the battles, their reactions, and their struggles. Of course, a great deal of this was done in the editing room, but it is a valuable movie to watch to give you an idea of how to pace your battles. Branagh's use of slow motion is some of the best that I've ever seen.

Another good movie for battle scenes is *Willow*. Again this is a fight between good and evil. In the final fight, the action bounces between the big battle and Willow's struggle with the witch for the baby Elora. The pace is fast, but still varied enough that the audience is never left wishing for a moment to catch its breath. As the movie contains a fair amount of humor, it is included in the fighting to break up the seriousness and gore.

I stated earlier in this chapter that not all battles are on the battlefield. Many heroes must fight inner battles... like a hero in a romance or a drama. But if you are writing a big battle scene ask yourself: Is it NEEDED? Am I putting it in the story because that's how Fantasy is? If you answered, "Yes" to the last question, go back and read Chapter 1 again, please!

Movies without Big Bloody Battles

If you have to have a fight in a smaller, intimate Fantasy, a brief skirmish between a few people is enough. *Ladyhawke* utilizes a smaller cast of extras with well-choreographed fight scenes. There is no need for a large physical battle because the story doesn't support such a display of arms. What is more important in a movie such as *Ladyhawke* is the inner battle the hero, and those around him, experience.

A hero's inner struggles in Fantasy are as varied as the struggles of characters in other stories, such as:

The knight, Bowen, in *Dragonheart* is a man whose soul is rooted in "the old code" of knightly honor. When the prince he mentored discards the code, Bowen suffers a crisis of faith.

In *Ladyhawke*, Captain Navarre is a soldier used to protecting others. Yet, he cannot protect the woman he loves against an evil curse.

In *The Indian in the Cupboard*, young Omri learns that no matter what you want to do, you have to take other people's needs into consideration.

Beauty and the Beast has one of my favorite inner battles. As all old fairy tales are morality tales, this story asks the viewer (or reader) to examine her ideas of what true beauty is. Is it what's popular (anorexia, collegin lips, big hair) or is it that inner light that makes a person truly beautiful? Yes, in Disney's animated version there are fights and chases, but, in the old Jean Cocteau's version, you get more of the real story, the real inner conflict.

I know a woman who loathes Fantasy and says that *The Lord of the Rings Trilogy* has too many battles. She looked upon the movies as being nothing more than one fight after another. Don't ask me why she went to them, I don't know. I admit, however, that her observation is, in part, true. I wish that this epic tale could have contained more of the character development that was in the books, but it is almost impossible to give all the characters their due. If you can look past the physical battles, there are many inner battles going on: Frodo fights the ring trying to overpower his basic goodness; Aragorn, has many struggles, from his love for Arwen, whom he must let go, to the fact that he is Isildur's heir; Gandalf is grieved that little Frodo must bear the ring of power.

When you embark upon your first Fantasy spec script, think about your characters. Create biographies for them, get to know them, how they feel, what they like, what they dislike. Treat them as you would any other character in any other genre and understand their inner struggles. When you finally sit down to write the story, remember all these qualities and include them so that, despite any large bloody battles that might be in the movie, you still have real people to which a real audience can relate.

Comments by Dameon Willich, Fight Instructor
All the following questions about combat and battles in Fantasy have been answered by **Dameon Willich**, an award-winning

Fantasy artist and actor/combatant, as well as director of The Seattle Knights and the Seattle Knights Academy of Armored Combat. His love of history, horses, and teaching have combined over the last 20 years in teaching the art of combat for stage, screen, and theatre in the round. Dameon's art work has appeared on book covers and *James Bond*, *Avatar*, and *Return of the Warlord* comic books. He is also one of the artists for the game: *Magic: The Gathering*.

Question: *As a teacher of steel combat, what are some of your pet peeves in the movies that you see?*
"The total lack of historical application of combat techniques. Primarily in the Western culture techniques. Also, in movies, the majority of the actors never really wear real armor, so they are bounding around doing moves that real armor does not allow you to do. A fully armored knight would NEVER attempt a full lunge in the Italian fencing method... he would not be able to maintain balance and recover if he missed the blow, leaving himself open to a counter strike. There are many fight books that have been translated, the Fiore and Tal Hoffer works primarily, and some are actually being used these days to rectify some of these issues.

Another really fun point is how the heroes always take off their helms... so the audience can see them. Most warriors would always wear a helm first and foremost, even if other armor was not available. Helm and shield, then spaulders or paulderns (shoulder armor). Most of the deathblows in close combat are from a high strike breaking the collarbone. Death was usually from drowning on their own blood, if they did not die from the initial shock of the blow. Wounds are another peeve... most people in the movies are always fighting on without any concept of shock. I think that I like that in a movie because I really do not want my entertainment that realistic, and I want my heroes heroic. But there should be some basis of reality. The best Fantasy stories are those that are written close to reality.

The final thing that I think bothers me the most is that the Fantasy "knights" are always stuck on horses that were not around in the Middle Ages. The primary warhorses of the age were the Andulusians and cross breeds from those and Arabs and Spanish Jennets. The GREAT Norman horse was not that big. Paintings and horse shoes from the period bear this out."

Question: *Which three movies do you think have the best combat (hand-to-hand and otherwise) and why?*
"My favorites are:
1. *The Three Musketeers/Four Musketeers*. The choreography was done by William Hobbs, considered to be the best at the trade. He also did a great Napoleonic period movie called *The Duelists* that was superb. Mr. Hobbs does a lot of fun, fantastical fight choreography that also has a basis in reality movement. His recent *Count of Monte Christo* has a great knife fight in it, as well as the small sword duel at the end.

2. *The Mask of Zorror* — again, it was fun! The fight scenes are great and they are based on reality moves, much like *Princess Bride*, which is also fun, and a lot of work went into it, but the "quotes" did not match up to the moves. Although both of these are later period movies, they have great action sequences.

3. All three of *The Lord of the Rings*. These movies are so recent

that the fight work had all of the previous craft to draw on. Bob Anderson was the lead choreographer, but there were a lot of folks involved who had input into the fight scenes. The stunt crews wore armor and took hits that were well defined and can be viewed even in slow motion. The large battle scenes were great with a lot of quick cuts just like in *Braveheart*, allowing the scenes to actually appear chaotic and realistic. There were some spots where the movement became too repetitive, like in Boromir's death fight, but all in all, I have to rate them as some of the best."

Question: *From a historical point of view, what would you like to see more?*
"More actual fight work that is based on the fight books from Fiore and Tal Hoffer, or Monte, or any of the great works of the late period BEFORE the decline of armor. I would also like to see actual armor used. Train the actors to wear it and move in it so that it becomes more real. Use extras and stunt crews that wear armor regularly, and they will add a lot to the whole experience. Also, use people who actually can ride horses in the horse scenes."

Question: *Any general comments on the state of combat in current, and earlier, movies?*
"Like all of the art, the combat choreography is improving. I personally do not agree with the recent oriental influence that has brought the "Buckets of Blood" syndrome to our movie culture. I do not feel that heads being lopped off and blood spurting all over is necessary for the story to be told. *Kill Bill* had some great fight work in it, and there is no getting around that fact. Even with the recent wirework and CGI work that has infiltrated our

movie craft, the choreography is being ramped up to meet the audience's demand. Actor/Combatants can still perform great fights in real time, safer and better than we did in the previous decades. I feel that the "special effects" or FX have, at times, ruined the craft instead of helping it, but that is just MY opinion.

One last comment, I am in this industry to entertain and educate. I love the work that I do, and I love the fact that there are folks out there who want to help improve it. When I see errors in a movie like *TimeLine*, all I have to do is remember how far we have come in just the last 10 years and I can really appreciate what I am seeing. Also, I know from my own experience in the film industry, that what may have been shot in 20 takes may not be what ends up on the film. Often the best action footage is never seen. Editing often has ruined a great film, but also has made films great!"

An Exercise

Write a full, three-to-five page bloody battle scene in novel form. If you have to go over the page count, do so, but make sure it's as complete as possible. When you're finished, break it down into scenes and then break the scenes down. Now reconstruct it but keep it to its absolute barest minimum, even if it's only a few words, like a log line. Does it convey the full battle? If not (and I doubt it will) go back into what you've cut and pull out everything you feel is important. Reintroduce it back into the scenes little by little until you've got a solid battle scene.

A Recommendation

Some of the best battles scenes I've ever read in novels are those written by Bernard Cornwell, author of the *Sharpe's Rifles* series (made into BBC TV-movies starring Sean Bean). He's also the author of the Arthurian trilogy comprised of: *The Winter King*, *The Enemy of God*, and *Excalibur*, and the novel *Stonehenge*. You can find out more about him and his books at: *http://www.bernardcornwell.net/* I recommend his work highly.

CHAPTER 9

RELIGIOΠ
İF YOV HAVE A ΠΟΠΚ,
THERE SHOVLD BE A CHVRCH

Fantasy films placed in "olden times" usually have holy men (or women) in the scripts. Stories in a Central European setting often have a tonsured Christian monk or pagan priest(ess), Asian films have the monks and nuns of the different religions, and movies about aboriginal societies have shamans or witch doctors. Films in a more modern era, such as *Field of Dreams* or *Big*, rarely have clerics and, because of that, most of this chapter deals with the High Fantasy, Sword and Sorcery, or Fairy Tale type stories.

Religions in Fantasy are usually based on ancient practices that the author has — hopefully — researched. It's also a possibility that they're an amalgam of religions practiced today, i.e., the author writing what he knows. Detailed information regarding the religion (ancient or new) isn't needed in the script unless a particular part of it affects the story, such as a sacrifice, or the hero going off in the wilds for two weeks dressed only in a loincloth and armed with a kitchen knife.

Sometimes all you need to convey the essence of a religion is a costume. A classic friar's robe and cowl is similar, but different, from pagan robes. Costume is of course, the realm of costumers

and they'll know the difference when you write something akin
to the following:

Ext. Dirt Road — Day
Sweat glistens on Friar Tuck's tonsured pate as his little donkey
ambles down the road. Dust clings to the Friar's robes and san-
daled feet.

And:

Ext. Dirt Road — Day
Mystic Harloch's robes billow around him as his pointed hat
flops with every stride of his speedy horse.

Sometimes all you need to convey a religion is the costume. Dragonheart *(1996)*

The right costumes will nudge the audience to assume which
established religion (or Earth religion) the character practices.

Religions in our own world have ever-changing faces. Those of
long ago are rarely practiced now and those practiced today

may fall by the wayside in the next thousand years. This constant change of man's beliefs can play a large part in a script. TV's *Merlin* had the Goddess Mab working very hard to regain her place in the people's hearts over the encroaching Christian religion. This poses an interesting point of view: Do gods cease to exist if they are no longer worshipped, or do they sit around and wait to make a comeback when the time is right? And, if so, where are they? Does the cosmos have a giant green room somewhere for gods and goddesses awaiting their cues to re-enter stage left? In Chapter 2, Research, I mention Anne S. Baumgartner's book *Ye Gods!* as a quick reference guide to ancient religions. It doesn't hurt to do a little research into the gods who have been worshipped by the peoples of Earth.

In Fantasy, there are basically two religious factions: Good and Evil. Demons = bad, Angels = good. Gods and goddesses can be either. Fortunately, in Fantasy, the good gods are distinguishable from the bad ones: The good ones do good work, the bad ones do bad work. Gray areas exist only to help develop plot twists. Witches and wizards also are either good or evil, as in Glinda the Good Witch and The Wicked Witch of the West.

The more reality-based your story; the more it will affect the reality of the religion you include. In *Ladyhawke*, we know that the religion of the evil bishop USED to be Catholicism because the monk, Father Imperius, mentions that the holy church in Rome split with the bishop over his "dark" practices.

Suffering from PCism and afraid to offend anyone by making up a religion that's a little too close to one that already exists (and thus incurring the wrath of its members)? Depending on how old you are, you should know by now that no matter what you do, you're going to make someone mad. It's unavoidable, especially when dealing with a subject as volatile as religion. But don't let that stop you from including a religious character in your story, *if you need him*. If you don't, don't waste script space on him. There are no rules that say a religious person has to be in a Fantasy. If you haven't put one in your script, but the director wants to include a monk in the background as an extra in a market scene, that's his decision, and nothing you need to worry about.

When you do include a religion (and religious character) in your story, never ignore the fact that all religions have structure. They have a set way of performing rites and rituals with specific rules of behavior. There are hierarchies and lay people within the groups and all the jealousies, politics, and communal squabbles that exist outside of the religious community exist within it, too.

How do you convey this hierarchy? In *The Lord of the Rings: The Fellowship of the Ring*, Gandalf tells Frodo that he is going to meet with the head of his order. In this one sentence the wizard establishes that he belongs to a sect with rules, a culture, and methods of promotion. These men aren't practicing their magical ways without guidance and controls. This is a perfect illustration of how you needn't go into great detail about a religion and its followers. One well-written line will do it all.

Religious figures in Fantasy usually travel four main roads:

1. He (or she) is a very nice person and helps out whenever possible, sometimes providing comic relief.
2. He (or she) is a vile person and will do everything he can to ruin whatever is going on.
3. Religious factions hinder the hero's journey.
4. The hero's journey is the result of religious factions.

The Sorcerer & Religion

Sorcerers often have a religious connection with an obscure (or made up) god — usually referred to as "the old ways." Sometimes they wander through the world you've created or they take a very active part in the daily life of its inhabitants. They can be loved, or hated. They can be charlatans, pretending to place spells and provide potions, or they can be real and help the citizenry. In many books and movies they are scholars and scientists, studying everything from the people of the world to its flora and fauna. In our own "olden days" most scientists and scholars were considered witches and sorcerers because of their scientific studies, especially if they were interested in alchemy. Their curiosity in the unknown often was considered heresy.

Separation of Church and State

I have yet to see a separation of church and state in a Fantasy story. Keep in mind I haven't read every Fantasy book published nor have I seen every Fantasy film made, so there may be a book or movie out there in which a separation does exist. For the most part, however, the church (pagan or not) plays a huge part in the governments of Fantasylands. There are several scenarios that exist within this non-separation, here are but a few:

1. The king's chief advisor is a cleric (magical or not) and is a good person but:
   a. He's been framed and labeled a traitor.
   b. He's been killed and replaced by someone bad.
2. The king's chief advisor is a cleric who's been plotting against him.
3. A family member of the king has taken up with a nasty cleric (everything from a fanatic to a demon) and has been twisted to act against his king.

The list of possible plot lines available when church and state are tied in an endless knot is incredible. However, tread lightly with the subject as it has been done countless times and you risk turning your story into yet another rehashing of formulaic Fantasy.

The Sacrifice

What would a chapter on religion be without mentioning the sacrifice? Ask people what they think a sacrifice looks like in a Fantasy movie and they most often will say there will be a beautiful, young, female virgin on a stone alter with a knife positioned over her ample, heaving bosom. In addition, the person wielding the knife will be a wildly insane cleric or witch who has deviated from all that is good and decent. I have to admit, that is, indeed, what you often see.

There is nothing wrong with including a sacrifice (or attempted sacrifice) scene in your script, but before you do, ask yourself if it's really, really, REALLY necessary? The scene I just mentioned above is straight out of cliché central. If your script can't exist without a sacrificial scene, please try to find another way of showing it. And while I'm at it: Why does the sacrificial virgin HAVE to be female? I'm all for equality of the sexes when it comes to a good old-fashioned sacrifice scene.

Purpose of Religion

Before you include a religion or religious person in your story ask yourself this: What purpose does religion play in my story? Will it move the story forward? Will it stop it dead? Do the people in the story NEED to have a cleric, be he pagan or not? Remember, supplication of a deity is usually done to:

1. Ask for favors.
2. Ask for cures to illnesses.
3. Prevent something bad from happening.
4. Cause something good to happen.
5. Meddle in love affairs.
6. Provide guidance.

If your characters don't need help in this way, leave out the religion.

Never Include a Religion if ...

You've got a bone to pick and you're going to use your script to do it. Believe it or not, I've read spec scripts in which it was clear, early on, that the writer had a skewed idea of — and an idea to skewer — a religion (whether established or obscure). Unless you're producing your script yourself, or you have people who have asked you to write to their specifications, don't slam another religion, mainstream or otherwise. I'm not saying this because you risk offending someone but because a great many stories written with the specific purpose of slamming someone or something come off as preachy diatribes and nothing else. I really shouldn't have to mention this, but I've seen it often enough that I am.

An Exercise

Go over a list of Fantasy movies, books, and stories with which you're familiar. If there are religious characters included, examine their importance. Are they advisors to the heroes or to people in power? Do they move the action forward? Would the story be better, or worse, if the characters were not there?

If the books or movies didn't have religious figures in them would they be better if there had been some? If you're currently working on a Fantasy script and you have a minor character with a religious background in it, imagine the story without him/her. How does it change the story? Is it better or worse? Now ask yourself this: Did I create this character because of what I've seen in other movies, thinking that there had to be a religious character, or because I know that my story NEEDS to have one?

CHAPTER 10

POLITICS
YOU CAN'T HAVE POLITICAL UPHEAVAL WITHOUT POLITICAL DISSENT

Someone once asked me what politics had to do with a Fantasy story. I simply said, "Everything." Why? Because every story is political; from two suitors vying for the same person, to corporate personnel jockeying for promotions, politics is politics. We may tend to think of politics as two people stumping for votes, but the political scene of a Fantasy story (or any other story) doesn't have to be about government. It can be strictly personal.

In *The Princess Bride*, Humperdinck (Chris Sarandon) wants to start a war with Gilder by making it look like someone from Gilder killed his fiancé. Yes, this is government politics, but quickly turns into a contest between Humperdinck and Buttercup's (Robin Wright) true love, Westley (Cary Ewles.) In *It's a Wonderful Life*, Mr. Potter (Lionel Barrymore) has been trying for years to close down George Bailey's (Jimmy Stewart) business. His take-over bids are both business and personal politics.

You can use all manner of business, governmental, and personal politics in a Fantasy story. In addition, politics will be affected by the region (climate and geography) era, and culture of the world you have created.

Climate and Geology

In our real world of today, what are the politics of fossil fuels such as oil? Extensive, right? Now consider the wild political games behind the Spice and the scarceness of water in the science fiction classic *Dune*. Our physical surroundings can, and do, affect the politics in our lives and it shouldn't be any different for the politics in our stories.

Era

Again, as in real life, politics vary from era to era depending on the focus of the times: war, famine, prosperity, and civil rights, to name a few. Arthur spent much of his time trying to unite England. To help achieve this end he developed the round table, a brilliant stroke of political savvy.

Culture

Mores and manners are at play in any political arena. What one culture considers an insult another considers politeness. Consider the following:

There is a story, some say it's true, some say it's legend, that involves Gráinne (Grace) O'Malley, the Irish pirate queen. In 1593, she presented herself in the court of Queen Elizabeth to secure the release of her son from an Irish prison. It is said that when she met with Elizabeth, being fresh off a sailing ship where it had been cold, her nose began to run. Elizabeth politely handed her one of her royal handkerchiefs. Gráinne blew her nose and, as was her people's custom, promptly threw the soiled handkerchief in the fire. Elizabeth's attendants were appalled at this disdainful treatment of a royal gift. Elizabeth, the consummate diplomat, understood that there was no insult intended. However, had it been anyone else, the gesture might have been taken as rudeness personified. Whether the story is true or not, I can't say. I'm not a historian. I've heard from some people that it is true and I've heard from others that it is not. Either way it is: a) a fun little story, and b) an excellent example of cultural differences and the potential for political misunderstanding. Can you imagine what might have happened had Elizabeth been as insulted as her attendants?

Of course, these are a few of the external incentives that affect politics. What about the internal ones? What motivates your characters to enter the political games that are being played around them?

Political Incentives

The following is a list of some of the most important components at play in politics.

1. Power
2. Greed
3. Jealousy
4. Lust
5. Love
6. Hate

Power

The king (or ruler) is dead; long live the new king, whomever he may be. The story possibilities that exist when a king has died, be it naturally, during war, or at the hands of another, are limited only by your imagination. A few conflicts that can, should, or will surface are:

1. Sibling rivalry: Son against son, son against daughter, daughter against daughter, bastard son against legal son, bastard daughter against legal son/daughter, bastard child against bastard child (whether or not the king has legal heirs).

2. Familial rivalry: Queen against queen dowager, queen against legal heir or bastard heir, queen against mistress, vying uncles, aunts, brothers, or sisters, parents, 5th cousins thrice removed, ad infinitum.

3. Kings and rulers in different countries.

4. Under-noblemen such as dukes, barons, and knights vying to take over from an heirless king or to oust the heir.

5. Depending on how large a role religion plays in the kingdom, the struggle for the ear of the reigning monarch (not to mention the throne itself) can provide delicious intrigues. There is nothing as ominous as scurrying monks in the halls after a king has died.

6. Magic Men and Women.

    a. The king is dead due to a curse or other magical means, in which case the resident sorcerer/magician must struggle with powers of evil to bring things right.

    b. Perhaps the resident magician himself is the one who did the dirty deed in a take-over bid.

7. The sniveling, mincing bean counter in the back room with the motive and opportunity to make sure the king and the rest of his family is dead so he can grab all the power.

There is no end to the political possibilities in the fight to choose a new leader. The whispers in the hallways create havoc, causing people to choose sides, dump allies, and develop counter intrigues. In this atmosphere, the kingdom could be open to anyone taking over, even the kitchen maid, and wouldn't that result in an interesting tale? Not sure? Don't forget, as legend goes, an untried boy pulled the sword Excalibur from a huge stone and was then recognized as king.

What do you do with a ruler who's lost his faculties? This is a sub-plot in *The Lord of the Rings: The Two Towers* and *Dragonheart's* sequel, *Dragonheart, A New Beginning* (aka *Dragonheart II*). A close advisor in any circle of power (think Rasputin with the Romanovs) is always to be suspected of a take-over plot, or, if he isn't inclined to take over, he may be the target for betrayal by others seeking power. This power struggle isn't limited to kings and sorcerers. It is very evident in the film *Big*, with all the ladder climbers in the toy company.

But how is power obtained? Usually with the help of the following emotions:

Greed

It's human nature to covet what others have. A bigger house, a better stereo system, smarter kids, whatever the guy next door has, his neighbor wants. You can see it in the debt load carried by the average citizen in the United States today. If greed is so prevalent in real life, why shouldn't it play havoc with the characters in a Fantasy script?

As much as we hate to admit it, we've all experienced greed at one time or another. We've fantasized how fun it would be to walk into a favorite store, look around and say, "I'll take it all," even when we know we don't need it all. There's no particular angst behind this feeling, just good advertising. So if we don't have to have angst behind our greed, a character doesn't necessarily need it, either. Think of all the things your character can be greedy about! Everything from golden goose eggs to Dalmatian coats. A greed-motivated character can be deliciously wicked and over the top, or pathetically sad. Make sure, however, that he's not a caricature.

Jealousy

Ah jealousy! What wonderful political intrigues are available when jealousy runs amok through the corridors of the castle or corporation. Sister against sister, wizard against wizard, peasant against king, king against peasant, the possibilities are infinite. It's a motivation most of us can relate to and one that can strike the most reasonable person in any world.

What is jealousy? The simple explanation I found in the dictionary is that one person is resentful of another person. The reasons for the resentment are as varied as the people experiencing jealousy. I'm short and chubby, and I'm never jealous of a tall, willowy blond when she sashays past me in a restaurant. We're both the product of genetics. However, the fact that she can chow down on a big ol' banana split (with gusto!) has been known to produce a slight undershade of green in my complexion.

The most used jealousy situation in fiction is, of course, the love triangle. May I bring up *Ladyhawke* again? The bishop wants

Isabeau but she loves Navarre so the bishop's jealousy (desire to possess, in this case) drives him to curse the lovers. If he can't have Isabeau, no one can.

In the many retellings of the Arthurian legend, Morgana Le Fay's all-consuming jealousy of her brother drives her to incest, the product of which is a son. The son then turns against his father so that he, and ultimately his mother/aunt, can rule.

Although not technically a Fantasy (except for one episode), the delightful Rowen Atkinson TV series *The Black Adder*, follows the exploits of Edmund Blackadder, a young man driven to driveling distraction by the fact that his brother, Prince Harry, is the favored son. It doesn't matter that Harry is older and in line for the throne through the rules of ascension. Edmond's jealousy and greed drive him onward, so that he is forever trying to usurp his brother's position. His failings are epic in proportion and present a medieval Wiley Coyote trying every trick possible to land the Road Runner. Of course Prince Harry is every bit as sweet as the Road Runner is.

Jealousy can strike anyone, or any beastie at any time. Just ask someone with more than one pet. Your beloved babies ignore you, until one of them decides to sit in your lap; then they're all vying to be the center of attention.

In the real world, for the most part, jealousies blow over and that's where it ends. But in a Fantasy story jealousy can be taken farther, leading into betrayal, war, murder, and banishment.

Lust

What would authors do without this wonderful human emotion? And it covers so much: sexual lust, the lust for power, position, wealth, and fame. One would think it's the driving force behind all the other components listed above, and it may well be.

It takes a strong person not to give in to his desire. We're all familiar with sexual lust and the possibilities it brings to a story, but what about the lust for power and position? Countries have been plunged into wars and millions of lives ruined just so one man can hold the key to almighty power in his hand. The lust for wealth goes beyond mere greed and eventually destroys lives and personal relationships, as does the lust for fame.

If you want to enhance your characters normal desires, add a little lust to the mix and see if it doesn't take them to a newer level. The added lust may be what you need to move your story along. How? Imagine the following: Young stable boy Damian wants to be the stable master to the king. He's determined to reach his goal so he works hard to obtain it. You can fabricate a good story about a nice young man out of this idea. Add an overwhelming lust for the position to the story and the nice young man becomes possessed. Not only does he work hard at his job, he now starts undermining the other stable boys and even the stable master himself. And who's to say he'll stop at stable master once he's obtained the position? Lust is a delusional emotion.

Love

Ah, what people do for love. Sometimes it's good, sometimes it's bad. Heroes lay down their weapons and heroines agree to marry ugly toads if it will keep their true loves safe. Outsiders often use the love of two people to their own advantage and twist everyone's life upside down and sideways. People also kill in the name of love. Add politics to love and expect to be surprised.

In the political arena, love comes in many forms: intimate-sexual, intimate non-sexual, friendship, familial (mother and child, parents, grandparents, etc.), love of country, riches, religious love, love for a pet or an activity or power.

Every form of love produces a different political motivation and, of course, different political actions and effects. Here is an example: A father loves his son, but his love for his country may motivate him to expose his son when he finds out the young man is a traitor.

Love can create and solve problems. But it's best if it first creates the problems, and then sees them through to their usual happy endings.

Love Interrupted

What happens when love ceases to exist? Although not fiction, the political ramifications of a monarch such as England's Henry VIII should give you a very good idea of what you can do in a Fantasy story. And, of course, Love Interrupted usually ends in:

Hate

Love may, as it's said, make the world go 'round, but Hate does a grand job of spinning it off its axis. The basic reasons for hate are as varied as the people who experience it. Quite often hate is the result of jealousy, someone else's power, someone else's greed, and certainly, someone's lust. Write a character who hates with a cold, calculating mind and you've got a bomb waiting for the match to light its fuse.

Hate can motivate a character to manipulate everything and everyone around him. He can hide his hate behind a façade of gentile affability, or clinging uncertainty while he plots and plans his vicious schemes.

As bad as all the other emotions, unwisely used, can be, hate is the one that is most destructive and leaves the author with a slight dilemma at the end of his story: Does the character who hates learn to put aside his hate at the end (i.e., experiencing a character arc) or is he left to wallow in his misery while the characters around him experience an arc? You have to decide which ending is the most satisfying.

No matter what you write, be it a Fantasy filled with armies and battles, or two lovers trying to stay together, politics, in one form or another, will have a part to play in your story.

An Exercise

Pull out a current newspaper or news magazine and search through it for every article that you think pertains to politics, from election news, to people being promoted at a local company. You're looking, for the most part, at the end of the story, so now back track and try fabricating the politics behind the story you hold in your hands.

CHAPTER II

ROMANCE
AND MAYBE A LITTLE SEX?

There is something different about Romance when it's in a Fantasy story, and it's not the magical element. It's as if it's nobler, more ethereal. It's as if we truly believe (and most importantly, WANT to believe) that the beautiful couple in love will live happily ever after and never worry about taking out the garbage the day after the wedding.

The Fantasy romance suffers all manners of interruption; from rivals to curses to stepparents, but it always wins out. Romantic couples in Fantasies exist as one. Sometimes they put up a good show of fighting love, but that doesn't last long. Theirs is an attraction that usually happens the moment they see each other, and the audience recognizes it. Outside influences may stop them from acknowledging it, but true love cannot be denied. Other suitors may appear, temptations, suspicions, and jealousies come and go, but always, the lovers return to each other.

It's interesting to note that sex is rarely part of romance in a Fantasy movie. If anything, intercourse is used to sully the noble ideal. Forgive me; once again we turn to the famous (infamous?) Pendragon family: Uther lusted after Igraine and had intercourse with her while her husband was being murdered. Arthur was the result of the union and Morgana Le Fay, his half-sister, tricked

him into having sex with her. Mordred was born of that inces-
tuous union and he tore apart the Round Table. He was inad-
vertently aided in the destruction when Guenevere and
Lancelot gave in to their lust and committed adultery against
Arthur. As Sir Walter Scott said: "Oh, what a tangled web we
weave when first we practice to deceive."

Love conquers all in Ladyhawke *(1985).*

It would seem as if sex can't be part of a Fantasy unless it
results in doom and death. Of course, that's not entirely true…
but keep in mind that Fantasy often deals with the archetype.
However, if lovers have been lovers for a long time and are, in
fact, married with an adorable child playing at their feet, sex is
no longer nasty but an extension of their love. Go figure.

The more modern-era Fantasies skirt the sex issue, too. You know it existed in *It's a Wonderful Life* because George has children, ditto *The Mummy Returns*, *Practical Magic*, and *The Addams Family*. Nevertheless, you rarely see anything except its result, i.e., adorable children or, doom and destruction.

I know one shouldn't assume anything, but in this case I'm willing to go out on that shaky old limb and assume that sex is often left out of Fantasy movies because production company executives don't believe adults love the genre. Therefore, they're focused on keeping the film's PG-13 rating. Because of this we see an impassioned kiss and, occasionally, the moments leading up to the act and the moments after it and that's it. Makes me wonder if the executives know that sex *is* included in many novels, sometimes graphically? Whether you like sex in Fantasy or not is a personal preference. I don't, but then I'm a well-known prude. As a genre, Fantasy is ever evolving, so I'm not going to say sex will NEVER be in a mainstream Fantasy film. Notice I say, "mainstream." I would be remiss in not mentioning that there is a sub-genre known as Erotic Fantasy. You should know it exists and does have a following, if you want to write for it.

I find the lack of sex a little funny considering that ancient mythology runs rampant with it. The Greek and Roman gods coupled regularly with Earth folk, which gave us heroes like Hercules, and aboriginal peoples often tell of gods having intercourse with local villagers. Of course, in the blacker arts, the stories of succubi and incubi serve to warn all against impure thoughts and desires. Again, this casts the sex act in an evil light.

As much as sex is NOT part of filmed Fantasy, romance plays an extremely important role. Why else would an injured knight enter a joust but to save his fair lady from being paired with a drooling, pestilent pile of putrilage such as the evil Black Knight? (Cue the cackling hag in the background, please.) Why else would love spells and potions be bought and fortunes be sought, if not for romance and love? Can you imagine *The Princess Bride* without hearing "As you wish?" I can't.

Romance in a Fantasy is everything you want it to be in your own life. Ditto for the audience. And that's how you should approach it when you write it. Think of it as: Noble, Undying, Ethereal, Timeless, Forever, Exquisite, an Unbreakable Connection, and any other flowery, over-the-top description you can think of. The loving couple isn't just miserable if they're apart, they grieve. Every moment together is poignant, every moment apart heart wrenching. (Can't you just feel those enraptured sighs from the theater seat behind you?)

Filmed Fantasy romance has a rather large bump in its winding road. Chemistry. No matter how good the script, the quality of the romantic interludes in the film is affected by the chemistry between the actors involved. It doesn't matter if they're both multiple Oscar winners; if that special "something" isn't there, love scenes won't ring true with the audiences. Unfortunately, there is nothing you, or any other writer, can do about the situation. What you must do is concentrate on writing the very best romantic scenes that you can and hope — and pray — that it will inspire a spark to ignite between the actors.

How do you write those fabulous scenes? Learn from others.

What do you feel are some of the greatest loves scenes ever filmed? Rent them and study them. Don't limit yourself to Romances; span all the genres, from Comedy to Adventure. Also, pay attention to the love stories of older characters such as the couples in *On Golden Pond* and *A Lion in Winter*. In movies such as these, you can see how love endures (and twists) through the years. Above all, make sure you concentrate on the characters, NOT the actors.

In these love scenes what qualities did the characters like about each other? What did they dislike, admire, understand, not understand, come to understand, or choose to ignore? What is it that brought them together, or pulled them apart? Can you look at what they're feeling and say, "Wow, I know that!" Or, "Wow, I want that!" Once you get a feel for the love scenes… and yes, it HAS to be by feeling, not by intellect, multiply it, magnify it, idealize it. Remember, the higher the ideal, the better.

Speaking of ideals….

Fantasy has given the men in this world an impossible ideal to follow: The knight in shining armor. Mention him to most modern woman and, even if she denies "buying into" that old-fashioned ideal, there will be a moment's glint of "I wish" in the back of her eyes. I've heard women refer to boyfriends and husbands as their "knights in shining armor" and I've also heard them mention rusting armor when those same boyfriends and husbands have not measured up to this impossible role model. Added pressure is applied when this ideal is portrayed by a hunky, handsome actor. Alas, I fear modern men will forever battle the specter of the romantic knight in shining armor.

An Exercise

I will be the first to admit that the wrong actor can change the level of romance in a movie. What I want you to do here is not so much an exercise, as a game. Pick your favorite romantic Fantasy movie and imagine a different actor in the hero's role. Not another "romantic" lead actor, but someone totally unlikely (in your eyes) for the part; maybe a goofy, gangly actor known for his comedic, inept roles. Be fair, however, and imagine him as he is in his other roles. As an example, Jean Reno is quite often the tough guy, so you would imagine him playing this romantic role as that tough guy for which he's known. (Even though he is not usually thought of as a romantic lead, many women found him very romantic in *Roseanna's Grave*, a fine testament to his acting skills.)

Once you've placed your unlikely actor in the role, how does the romance fare? You can try the same game with different actresses, too. Have fun. But remember, no matter what you write, you're not going to have control over casting, so write your best and hope it inspires the best in everyone else.

CHAPTER 12

FAMILY
THE PEOPLE FROM WHOM
MANY CONFLICTS ARISE

Yo, Corleone Family! Move over, you ain't got nuttin' on the intrigue of the courtly families of Fantasy.

Do you know a dysfunctional family? If you do, imagine what they would be like if one of them, or all of them, had the ability to turn their siblings, parents, or nosey neighbors into wart-covered toads. When it comes to battling families in the realms of magic, someone's eyebrows — and probably a whole lot more — are going to get singed.

Yo! Corleone Family! Move over! Willow *(1988)*

Ancient rules of succession lend themselves to wonderful familial plotting for a Fantasy writer's script. The most well-known rule is that of the first-born son taking over a throne when a ruler dies. That's why so many kings are hot to marry brides they hope will bear them male heirs. In a few ancient cultures, however, when a ruler's death placed the firstborn son on the throne, all his other sons were murdered. This eliminated challenges to the succession, especially if the ruler had more than one wife. History is filled with stories of ambitious second and third wives — and concubines — plotting for their own sons to rule. Dig around in this mother lode of information and you'll never run out of story material, especially when you add magic. However, as we've seen in drama after drama (especially from Shakespeare) a ruler doesn't have to be dead for people to start plotting a takeover.

Common Fantasy takeover plots don't always involve family members only. Sometimes a resident wizard is in on it; sometimes a trusted associate plots with a family member.

Takeover plots include, but are not limited to:

1. The firstborn son is nothing but a puppet, either because he's very young or he's misguided. The fight for the power behind the thrown starts here!
2. The firstborn son is: bad, stupid, a playboy, and any number of attributes that one would not want in a ruler. All eyes turn to the second son and how to oust the first or, the second son decides to mutiny.
3. The firstborn child is a girl. She steps aside for her brother but marries an unscrupulous man (arranged marriage) who has his eyes on the throne and plots against her younger brother.

These are but three stereotypical ideas. If you look into the ruling houses of any land across this globe that had a king, emperor, pharaoh, chief or sheik, you'll be able to find more scenarios from which to draw material.

Anything can set off scheming when it comes to a family. It doesn't have to be the quest for power, nor does it always have to be about the boys. Singer Loreena McKennitt used traditional lyrics in her song: "The Bonny Swans" to tell the tale of two sisters. The eldest drowns the youngest because she is jealous over the younger sister's suitor. The drowned sister turns into a swan. A harper then uses the swan's bones to craft a harp and when the instrument is played for the girl's family, it sings its sad tale and exposes the eldest sister and her murderous act.

Then, of course, we have all the stepmother stories of our youth. I remember being one of the first children in my small Wisconsin town to have a stepmother back in the 1950s. The kids at school would whisper, "You have a... *stepmother!*" We all knew from *Snow White* and *Cinderella* what stepmothers were like! They were evil and nasty and mine was probably plotting to turn me into a toad (not hardly). It was a bum rap for her, and for other very lovely people, and it continues today! In fiction, however, what better way to introduce a creepy stranger.

Audiences relate to dysfunctional families; unfortunately it's a subject of which many have first-hand knowledge. Think about your own family. Even if it is functional, do you have a member or two who always seems to curry favor with an older family member, usually an older RICH family member?

Don't restrict your story ideas to the fights within one family. Carry it further and have warring families ala Romeo and Juliet, or the Hatfields and the McCoys. Family conflicts can be found in all forms of fiction, from Westerns to Detective stories. Never hesitate to explore this avenue.

Stories don't have to center around a family in conflict. In *The Indian in the Cupboard*, Omri is given an old cupboard by his brother, and his mother has a key from her grandmother's key collection that just happens to fit it. In this story, the boy is surrounded by a loving and nurturing family. Ray Kinsella (*Field of Dreams*) is supported by his wife and daughter while he builds the baseball field; although he is in conflict with his brother-in-law.

In *Peter Pan* both Wendy and Peter come from loving families, but they disagree with their parents' plans for them. At first, neither one wants to admit that growing up is something that must happen, eventually. Once outside of their birth families, they create their own family group. Which leads me to another family dynamic: Friends and the people with whom you work.

Are not the men of *The Fellowship of the Ring* a family? They pull together to survive and care about each other. People who survive hardship and disaster often think of themselves as family. Men and women thrown together in war call their fellow soldiers "family." Gang members look at their gangs as families, as does organized crime, the police, and firefighters. Whenever you have a group of people who bond together for one reason or another, they become a type of family. There will be squabbles, hurts, and reconciliation, the same as in a genetic family.

While planning the family dynamics in your script look at all the variables available to you. You could have a character torn between his genetic family and his brothers-in-arms, or even between the genetic family and the family he's married into, or wants to marry into. As I said in this chapter's heading about families, they are: "… the people from whom many conflicts arise."

An Exercise

Make a list of the various conflicts that exist in families you know. They can be small (from children refusing to clean their rooms) to large like abuse and infidelity. Now toss out the big issues and pick a couple of the small, insignificant ones. I say this because the big issues get written about all the time. Pick a small issue and expand upon it, maybe like this:

Polly and her mother always squabble about Polly cleaning her room. The little girl doesn't want to do it and doesn't understand why it's such a big deal to her mother. The mother, on the other hand, doesn't want to tell Polly about the Dustus Mitus monster and what misery it can bring upon their household… and Polly's mother should know: when she was Polly's age she lost her younger brother to the monster and every day that Polly refuses to clean her room, her mother hears the footsteps of the Dustus Mitus grow louder and louder.

Whatever "small" conflict you come up with, sprinkle it with magic and loose your imagination. Who knows, you may have your whole Fantasy script right in front of you!

CHAPTER 13

LANGUAGES,
OR,
IS BIPPITY BOPPITY BOO NECESSARY?

Different Languages
INT: Castle Hallway — Day
In the shadow-filled hallway Prince Anono kisses Princess Tesasa.

Prince Anono
Bleomeo acknaga sheetata.
Princess Tesasa
Mena manna wappa, sango tumo wefafa
moanna!

If you were a reader for a production company, with this script in your hands, what would your thoughts be about this exchange? Hopefully nothing stronger than "HUH?" but my bet would be that you'd utter a few quick swear words and look for the wastebasket. That's why, if you're thinking of creating another language for your script I urge you to rethink your plans.

I know, I know, *The Lord of the Rings I-II & III* had tons of Elfish throughout the movie and used subtitles so people would know what the characters were saying. So what? You didn't write those movies. They're based on *books* that have been around for decades. You're working on a *script*, most likely a *spec script*. You want people to be able to read it without any interruptions in its flow. Even if you're a linguist and you've created the ultimate new language, you shouldn't put it in a script. Why? Because that smooth flow you want readers to experience will not happen if they have to stop and figure out what the heck your characters are saying. If you want them to speak in a different language, do the following:

INT. Castle Hallway — Day
In the shadow-filled hallway Prince Anono kisses Princess Tesasa. They speak in Tesasa's native language; subtitles read:

> Prince Anono
> I love you.

> Princess Tesasa
> My father's behind you and he has a knife!

The producer or director will take it from there. How they arrive at a language is up to them and whomever they hire to create it. After some research, I've learned from people in writer-director Stephen Sommers' offices that the language used in The Mummy and The Mummy Returns was translated "as much as possible" by an Egyptologist. I wasn't told what it was translated from, but it sounded terrific and never pulled me out of the story.

If you feel a language will add something extra to the story (the Elfish in The Lord of the Rings had a mesmerizing effect) and you feel a description is needed to get the correct feel of it, try this: Prince Anono's guttural language makes Princess Tesasa shudder, or: Princess Tesasa's soft, musical language charmed the rabid imp. A reader can relate to "guttural" and "musical" because there are languages here on Earth that have those qualities.

What about using a real language, like Welsh? Sure, you could do that, but why? Someone is going to understand it and hearing it will take him or her out of the movie. As much as I love opera I hate it sung in English because I lose focus on the music and concentrate on trying to understand the words. Do you really want people to focus on the language instead of your story?

If you absolutely INSIST on creating a full language, fine, do it, I can't stop you. But I do implore you, give the actors a break and create something they can wrap their lips and tongues around without too much trouble.

As to the words used in magic spells, I have an opposite view of using a different language in these instances. Go ahead and do it. Audiences expect to hear a strange language at this point in the script. It's what they're used to. Don't disappoint them. But, no matter what language you use for a spell, be it the one in which you're writing (English, French, Spanish, etc.) or something special you've created, make sure it is believable.

The *Harry Potter* movies use both Latin and made-up Latin. Again, these movies are based on books and I assume that J. K. Rawlings knew people reading the books would probably try to translate the spells. I should note here that I've a fair hand at reading and writing Anglo-Saxon Futhark Runes and you can bet I've translated what I've seen in *The Lord of the Rings* movies. What can I say, we Fantasy fans are like that! Don't believe me? You can find Harry Potter's spell words translated at: *http://www.harrypottermad.com/latother.htm.*

Latin (and a quasi-Latin) is always good for magic spells. Harry Potter and the Chamber of Secrets *(2002)*

If you do choose to make up odd little phrases and words for spells, here's an interesting piece of information you could put to good use in your script: It is thought, by some magic practitioners, that spells must be spoken exactly the same way each time they're said to insure the results are the same. Deviation will cause all types of problems, from a failed spell to a greatly altered result. An example: a Plain Jane wants to be beautiful and go to the ball at the palace. Her fairy godmother waves her wand and says something in a singsong voice and bingo; you've got a beauty on your hands and off she goes to the ball. Jane's such a hit at the ball she now has a hot date for next Saturday. Saturday rolls around and once more Jane asks her fairy godmother to twirl her wand and, just as the godmother gets to the last word in the spell, she sneezes. The result? Jane's date finds himself saddled with a two-foot hairy lima bean with purple eyes and a runny nose.

It's my personal opinion that special words for spells add to the fun of the movie. But keep the spells brief, and possibly understandable. Perhaps Jane's fairy godmother could have said something like: Maximus, Beautimus, Immetius. It doesn't take much for the ear to translate that to: Maximum Beauty Immediately. Short, but effective. This theory of incorrectly said spells resulting in nasty consequences was used to perfection in 1993's *Army of Darkness,* written by Sam Raimi and Ivan Raimi, and starring Bruce Campbell as the muddle-mouthed hero.

As I said, if you stick to your own language in the script and add the notation, "Speaks in Elfish" (or whatever language your character is supposed to speak), your script will do fine with the reader. Once it is purchased and in the hands of a studio, languages can be developed, bastardized, or not used at all and instead replaced with sayings such as: Bippity Bopppity Boo. Which, when you think about it, is pretty darned cute.

Quality of Language
English Through the Ages by William Brohaugh. Every writer should have this book, or one like it, on his shelf. It chronicles the origin of words, what their old meanings were and what they mean now. Why do I think it's important for you to have? I recently read a rant in the local newspaper's "Rants & Raves" column. This particular column was devoted to movies and one of the ranters wrote about how he hated hearing contemporary language used in period pieces. His particular rant concerned *Cold Mountain.* He had heard a current expression in the film and found it a distraction that took him out of the film. I willingly admit it, I agree with the ranter and his annoyance at the use of current language in period pieces. My involvement/investment in a movie is also destroyed by non-period language.

There are two exceptions, however: The TV series *Hercules*, and *Xena, Princess Warrior*. I wasn't thrilled, in the first episode of *Hercules*, to hear modern vernacular, but it was evident, very quickly, that the series were aimed at modern viewers and for the most part, they were very cleverly done. I also thought that maybe, even though the language was current, the series could spark an interest in ancient stories with a younger audience, so for these two reasons, I put my usual prejudice aside.

Obviously, with Fantasy, you have a little leeway in your choice of language. However, if the story is set in a very specific time period, do yourself a favor and double-check your words. Do they feel right? Do they fit with the times? Do they yank a viewer/reader out of the story because they're too modern and, thus, disrupt the flow of the story? When you spend enough time around Fantasy fans you will find many of them have a keen interest in history and words and are well educated, both academically and through self-study.

Several actor friends of mine have remarked on the almost Shakespearean quality of the language in *The Lord of the Rings*. Fortunately, Director Peter Jackson is extremely well served by his exceptional actors and their abilities to make their lines roll trippingly on their tongues. (Sorry, I couldn't resist that.) Not all movies will be as lucky. If the language in your script is too formal or archaic, it could sound very stiff and awkward in the mouths of lesser actors.

The writer, unfortunately, has little to do with casting, so he must concentrate on the following when creating dialogue:

1. Make it real and natural.
2. Make it fit (reasonably) with the time period.
3. Make it a joy for the actor.
4. Make it thrilling for the audience.
5. Prevent the characters from sounding alike. (Remember Yoda's speech pattern?)
6. Above all, make it believable.

Not all of the dialogue in *The Lord of the Rings* was Shakespearean. What was, was used judiciously, only when it heightened the emotions of the moment. At the same time, the more modern language was not in keeping with our current times. You didn't hear expressions like "Say what?" "Y'know." "Know what I mean?" "Whoa!" (except for stopping a horse). "Ya gotta be kidding!" or, one of my own favorites "kinda-sorta."

Should you be interested in mixing languages a little, author Laura Crockett's book: *Trippingly on the Tongue, A Booke of Instruction for Speaking Early Modern English* could be of some help. If you're any kind of a wordsmith, it is both fun and very informative.

An Exercise

Sit down and write a scene (three pages) with three different characters, each one speaking a different language. Make up each one of the languages. One soft and gentle, one guttural, one very strange. Rewrite the scene in your own language, using the "subtitles" direction.

After you finish both versions, put the scenes away. In a week, or even longer, go back and read them both. Now ask yourself: If you were a studio reader, which scene would you prefer to have cross your desk?

CHAPTER 14

MUSIC AND POETRY

Music

Since you have no control over the score of the movie made from your script, there is no need to include descriptions of music, unless the music has something to do with the story. This usually can be done quickly with one line such as, "Jason and the Argonauts fall under the spell of the beautiful song of the Sirens." Or, "The musicians in the tavern's corner play a jig." The director and composer will take it from there. You may not like their adaptation of the latest pop song as a jig, but if that's what they want to use, that's what they'll use.

If music and poetry are important parts of the script — perhaps your hero is a harpist, or the harp the hero plays is a living entity — you still needn't go into lengthy descriptions. Phrases such as "ethereal tones" or "discordant blasts," although some-what cliché, will work fine and leave no questions as to the type of music played. Keep it simple. At this point your script is for the reader, the producer, and the director, not the audience.

Poetry

Many Fantasy books include poetry. *The Dragonriders of Pern* series by Ursula La Guinn has ongoing Harper characters. They compose music and record the history of the inhabitants of Pern, much like the wandering minstrels of Old Europe. If your script has such a character in it and he has to recite a poem now and then, make sure it's a short one. I say short because, just as not all writers have epic poem talent, very few audience members want to listen to a 20-stanza poem about the capturing of an enemy's castle.

However, if you want to have a little fun with epic poetry and you have a harper at a feast going on and on about a huge battle, you could turn it into a running joke. But again, only in short snippets. Perhaps he starts his tale at the beginning of the feast. At first people pay attention but as the feast continues, like a piano player in a bar, the harper becomes background noise. The story progresses and two people walk past him with the following exchange:

Person One
This poem sounds like the last one.

Person Two
That's because it is.

There have been times when scripts have had supporting characters speaking in rhyme such as Pete Postlethwaite as Brother Gilbert of Glockenspur in *Dragonheart*. If you chose to do this, make sure you're good at it. There's nothing like bad rhymes (unless intentionally bad) to turn an audience off, so don't overdo it. You need to adhere to the following with the rhyming character:

1. They don't have large roles. (There are always exceptions to this.)

2. Make sure the rhyming is totally relevant to the character OR make sure it is highly important to the story.

3. Be consistent. If a character likes to speak in rhyme, make sure he does it all the time, or does it often enough that audiences can fall in to his rhythm quickly, so their viewing isn't disrupted.

Again, you can make a joke out of the rhyming; you can have people walking by the rhymer and offering words (not unlike people offering assistance to crossword puzzle fans) or even counter-rhyming just to throw him off.

As I said, poetry and music are often important in Fantasy stories, and there's no reason why they can't be part of a Fantasy film. But, if they don't further the story, i.e., they're just window dressing, a little will go a long way.

An Exercise

Make a cup of coffee or tea; pull up a chair and write your script's story in epic poem form. Write it in your own style, or Alfred, Lord Tennyson's *Idylls of the King*, or Edmund Spenser's *The Faery Queen*. It doesn't matter — just give it a shot. Have fun!

By the way, the dedication in Spenser's book is epic in itself:
"To the most high, mighty, and magnifice
Empress,
Renowned for piety, virtue and all gracious government,
Elizabeth,
By the grace of god
Queen of England, France, and Ireland, and of Virginia,
Defender of the faith, &
Her most humble servant
Edmund Spenser
Doth in all humility
Dedicate, present and consecrate
These his labors
To live with the eternity of her fame."

Wow! Go forth ye gentle writer and epicize!

CHAPTER 15

DETAİLS

A few years ago, I read the rough draft of a colleague's script. He knew the Fantasy genre, so the draft moved along at a decent clip and the story was interesting. Until I hit a small detail that stopped it all. In the story, a spoiled young princess demanded that her father build her a castle with parapets edged in Emeralds. When Daddy didn't comply she upped the anti and demanded a bigger castle with parapets edged in Amethysts.

Maybe it's because I once worked for a jeweler, or maybe it's because I'm a woman, but I knew that going from Emeralds to Amethysts was a bad case of downsizing. I couldn't shrug it off. I contacted my friend and asked him if he knew that Emeralds were precious stones and Amethysts were considered semi-precious? The princess should have asked for Amethysts first and then moved up to Emeralds. He didn't know this but, to his credit, he wasn't surprised when I told him this miniscule detail had blown my concentration. He understood the value of correct details and how they affect a reader or viewer's trust in the story.

And that's where incorrect details can kill a writer. Wrong details say the following:

1. You don't care.
2. You're not aware.
3. You're not serious.
4. You can't be trusted.

Correct details, however, say this:

1. You're thorough.
2. You do care.
3. You know what you're doing, and if you're not sure, you'll check it out.
4. You can be trusted.

It's a shame that one teensy-weensy little detail can stop everything, but it can and it does. Despite what some studio executives might think, today's audiences are smart and don't need dumbed-down movies. They're also much more sophisticated than the audiences of a few years ago. With CSI (Crime Scene Investigation) programs on PBS and network TV, scientific cable channels like Discovery, and the Internet, today's audiences are exposed to a great deal of information, including discussion groups about specific movies. Fantasy fans can pick out what is bogus and what isn't without missing a second. To them, details *aren't* like pearl-producing grains of sand in an oyster's craw. If they're wrong, they're ugly and insulting to the audience's intelligence.

But it's just a movie and they won't remember it, right?

Twenty-five years ago I saw an important ballet company perform *Swan Lake*. What do I remember about this critically acclaimed production? I remember the lead male dancer leaping across the stage with a huge run in his burgundy tights, and the little corps ballerina who'd forgotten to take off her leg warmers before going on stage. (And she was WAY in the back!) Thirty-five dollar tickets on a junior secretary's pay and that's all

I remember about a beautiful ballet? That's very sad and it points out that the cliché "the Devil's in the Details" is true.

I hear your protests now: "But this is a Fantasy script! Everything is make believe, who will know? Costumers will take care of the weapons and clothing. Set designers will handle scenic work. CGI will create incredible effects. Why do I have to worry about details, someone else will take care of them."

True, others will take care of them, but sometimes they won't get them right, so wouldn't it be nice if the right information was in the script in the first place? What you have to do is make your details important to the story.

If you've included a detail in a script that you're not sure about (my friend told me he hadn't been sure about the gems), take a moment to check it out. Selling a script is hard, so do EVERY-THING you can to make sure it's as perfect as you can make it. No matter what gets put up on screen, right or wrong, at least you'll know you did your best to make sure all the details were correct.

Remember Frodo's little sword "Sting" in *The Lord of the Rings*? Whether Tolkien thought his books would be made into movies, I don't know, but the fact that a Hobbit is too small for a big sword, plus Sting's ability to glow when Orcs are around, gives Sting a big purpose, so its smallness is a detail that will never be changed.

Do the same with your details as Tolkien did with Sting, and as my friend did with the gems. The jump from Amethysts to Emeralds (eventually) showed how greedy and spoiled the Princess was. And, I repeat: Never underestimate your audiences' knowledge, especially audiences of Fantasy Fans. They can be very forgiving if the story is good, but if there are too many mistakes they will be ruthless in their assessment and won't hesitate to get on the Web — and the several thousand Web sites devoted to Fantasy — to point out errors in the film.

If you still think you don't need to pay attention to the details, look at it this way: What could it hurt? A good, well-researched, and believable script will make you look good, and that's what you want, right?

An Exercise

Watch one of your favorite Fantasy films and take notes of the small details, from the flagons used at an inn, to the manner of dress worn by the characters to the food they eat, absolutely anything you think to include. See how the details enrich the story, from the ones that just fill out a scene to the ones that make a difference, such as the size of Frodo's sword. And, lastly, see if there are any that you recognize as "wrong."

CHAPTER 16

DESCRIPTIONS

When a slimy, crawling pink blob grabs your hero's foot, all you need by way of description is: A slimy, crawling pink blob grabs the hero's foot. The guys and gals in CGI don't need anything more. They've got very active imaginations down there and, depending on what the slimy, crawling pink blob ends up doing to your hero, you can be assured that the CGI people will create something that is as ugly as, or even more ugly, than you imagined.

In Fantasy novels, a great deal of paper is used on description, and with good reason, the author is translating what is in his mind's eye to the page so that you, too, can see what he is seeing. You already know that many a script (Fantasy and other genres) has seen an early death because of excessive descriptive passages. Which leaves the Fantasy writer with a dilemma, how does he translate what's in his mind's eye so the director can see it and, ultimately, get it up on screen? The answer is a short one: Brevity.

Think of your descriptive passages as loglines to the action. Haul out your adjectives and use them. Take, for instance, the following:

EXT. Road — Day
Jamie rides his horse down the road to the castle. Its gates hang by broken hinges. Birds nest in holes in the walls and a flash of

orange here and there attests to the proximity of a fox den. An eerie wail floats on the mournful wind that blows through the smashed parapets.

Your first reaction, I hope, is that this description needs to be cut down considerably. After all:

1. Jamie rides his horse to the RUINED castle.
2. An eerie wail is heard.

That's all the information you need, right? No. A "ruined" castle isn't always an old castle. It could be a new scene of destruction. However, this particular castle is an older ruin, so you need something to illustrate the fact, like the nesting birds and the fox family. But how to be brief? Try this:

EXT. **Ruined** Castle – Day
Birds burst from nests in the broken walls as a wail echoes behind its smashed parapets. Jamie stops his horse from backing away.

You've taken care of half your problem in your scene heading: **Ruined** Castle. The birds fleeing their nests in the walls show that the ruination isn't recent. The wail tells you something scary is behind the walls. And, lastly, you know Jamie has a horse on the road that leads to the castle. You've gone from fifty-seven words down to twenty-six. You could cut this down more by saying "Old ruined castle" in the heading and leave out the birds, but I left them in for two reasons, 1) the nests reinforce the age of the ruin and 2) to break up a tranquil scene, thus setting a "danger" mood. If you've ever been around a flock of birds as they've taken flight at the same time, the effect is quite startling. With the birds bursting from the walls the description says, "Something's going on." The use of "broken walls" confirms the "ruined castle" and "smashed parapets" say this isn't an abandoned ruin — "smashed" hints at a possible war. Some people might disagree with me in my assessment, so the choice is yours. One question the scene does, however, raise is: How did this castle come to its sorry state and what the heck is wailing behind its walls?

Two of the hardest things to describe in Fantasy are the beasties and magic rites. Yes, battles too, but they were covered in Chapter 8, so I'm not going to discuss them here.

How do you describe a beastie that is not a normal animal such as a cow or pig or calico cat? I like to draw it first. If you can sketch a little, try it. Draw the picture you're seeing in your mind, or, if you can't draw, ask a friend who can to help you out. Once you have a physical picture of the beastie in hand, start your rough draft description. Think of it as a modern day police report: height/size, weight, color of fur (or scales or skin), legs, (yes, no, several, few, etc.). You could make a list with descriptive passages after it:

1. Height/size: Big, beefy, humongous, gigantic, miniscule, tiny.
2. Weight: Heavy, skinny, slender, chunky.
3. Color of skin/fur, etc: green scales, brown fur, purple skin.
4. Legs: two, four, stubby, long and skinny, heavy, disjointed.
5. Distinguishing features: Torso ridged like a worm, blotches of pink and purple, green slime trail.

After you've created your description sheet, go through and find what works for you and what doesn't. Make sure you keep three things in mind: Keep it simple; you want the reader to catch on; the guys in CGI can do wonders. If you really want your green, scaly beastie with a ridged torso to have pink antennas (and you should have a good reason why he needs them) put that in, but you don't have to do much more. Keep it to just the facts.

Describing magic rites can be tough, too. How much is too much and how much is too little? My personal preference is to say something akin to: The magician mumbles a spell and throws ashes into the fire and poof! He's got a date for tonight.

Well, maybe I'm not that flippant, but the most important part of a magic rite on screen is not so much the rite, but what happens during and after it. If the magician is mixing a batch of a vile little potion, does he mix it all together and then bottle the finished product, or does it boil and bubble and turn five shades of chartreuse before it goes into the bottle? The boil and bubble and color would be great in your description because it's much more showy.

What you really want is some sort of result. You want that "poof!" But what if the "poof!" is going to happen later? No problem. After the rite, the magician simply says it will happen later. But this is boring, so something has to happen DURING the rite to give a little hint of what is to come. If the magician is evil and he's concocting a potion to be used against the hero, the following could take place as he works: a splashed drop of the potion causes a tiny spot on the counter to grow hair, or a pale purple glow comes from the potion's vial, or you can cut back and forth to the sleeping hero. With every ingredient added to the potion, he twists and turns in his bed. He sweats, or grips his weapon, or moans in agony. Make sure you're showing something going on while magic is being wrought and your audience won't be disappointed when the magician simply says: "THIS will produce results!"

An Exercise

I've already suggested this to you, but I'll do it again. Pull out paper and pencil and draw a beastie or a scene that you want to include in your script. Or, go ahead and pick a scene or beastie from an established Fantasy film. Draw it out and then, from the drawing in front of you, start picking out what is important and what can be passed over in the description. After you've done that, create as short and telling a description as you can.

CHAPTER 17

THE STORY
PART TWO

In Chapter 3, The Story — Part One, I told you not to worry if you came up with a story idea before you started thinking about your characters. I hold by what I said. But now, after going over all the stereotypes I can think of for characters and beasts and locations, etc., I'd like to continue with a few story ideas that I haven't covered in other chapters. They are:

The Prophecy

One story that runs throughout the world's peoples is that of the prophecy. From the ancient Greek play *Oedipus* to the current story of Neo in *The Matrix* (I consider this one of those movies that straddles the Science Fiction/Fantasy fence) the prophecy is a reoccurring theme. A person isn't always the subject of a prophecy, either. The Native American legend of the White Buffalo is an important prophetic tale.

Some of the ways a prophecy story is handled is:

1. The poor reluctant hero is clueless about whom he is.
2. The hero is wearing an amulet that sends the bad guy's minions into fits to get it. Of course, he has absolutely no idea how important the piece is.
3. The hero is usually a poor schmuck who doesn't know how to fight, etc., and has to be trained by other people around him.

4. "The One" is so inept that others despair of ever being saved. Of course, he proves up to the challenge, but only in the eleventh hour.

For the most part, we Fantasy fans enjoy these stories, and, if they're very well done, we ignore the fact that it is yet another prophesy tale. If anything, many of us add to the huge pile already in existence. I've even got a couple of unfinished scripts tucked away in my files that contain the very same cliché.

The Object

Of course, one of the first objects you think of is The One Ring from *The Lord of the Rings Trilogy*. There is also The Ark in *Indiana Jones*, the Holy Grail (both *Indiana Jones* and Arthurian legends), Pandora's box, Aladdin's Lamp, a fabulous jewel, a Rosetta stone, etc. Pick an inanimate object and you can create a story around it.

Ultimately the story is about the people around the object, but the object acts as another character dictating the behavior of every individual who comes in contact with it.

The Quest

When you think about it, every story is a "quest" story. In romance, the hero's quest is getting the girl; in crime, the detective's quest is bringing the criminal to justice, and, in Fantasy, the quest can be anything from rescuing the damsel to hunting down the swordsman who killed your father.

What the hero learns along the way while pursuing his quest is what, in the end, captures the audience. It is usually the sub-quest that is the true quest.

Sub-quest? In *Dragonslayer*, young Galen (Peter MacNicol) sets out to kill the dragon. That's his quest, he thinks. His sub-quest is his coming of age, both as a young man and as a wizard.

In *Willow*, little Willow's quest is to get the Princess Elora to safety. But the sub-quest is his self-realization.

Because Fantasy travels across all genres and all times, your chances of creating a Fantasy story that is unique and unusual are very good. Bet that's something you don't hear often! Yes, there will be similarities (remember that collective memory) but you can still build on them. And face it, a woman surfing in 17th century England has GOT to be a unique story, don't you think? (Please see page 95, #10, The Witch of Newbury.)

I hope much of the information that has been included in this book will provide you with both ideas and references on how to put your stories together. Unfortunately, Fantasies do have a reputation for having a formula, but I challenge you to change that stereotype.

What They Say:
What challenges do you feel a Fantasy script offers over other genres like mystery or drama?

Kathy Fong Yoneda: Script consultant/producer, author of *The Script-Selling Game: A Hollywood Insider's Look at Getting Your Script Sold and Produced.*

"Writing in the Fantasy genre offers a whole realm of choices and options that other genres may not have. It's a chance for a writer's imagination to take flight, to go places and experience new adventures. The hardest part about writing in this genre is reining in your imagination so viewers will still be enthralled with the adventure, but will also relate to it on some personal level, giving them a profound truth that touches them in an unexpected way."

Darragh Metzger:
"A good Fantasy script captures the audience's emotions just as any other good scripts should, while totally removing certain "rules" of reality that make the audience feel safe. Good Fantasy should stretch the bounds of reality and still make the audience believe in it. There is no other genre that offers that challenge. Nor does any other genre have the range to play in: after all, Fantasy can utilize the conventions of every other genre, while including elements denied every other genre. Quite simply, it's a limitless playing field."

CHAPTER 18

PUTTinG iT ALL TOGETHER

Boy, if you're still with me, you really are interested in writing a Fantasy script. Congratulations on your fortitude. I guess this means you're ready for the rules of Fantasy.

The unbending rule is: Be logical. There is logic even in chaos; it just takes a little longer to find it. So find the logic in your story and remember, with logic comes believability.

The liquid rule is: There are no absolutes. Heroes are not always stalwart and strong, beasties are not always mean and terrifying, and magic is not always a blue ball of flame.

What you want to aspire to: Create a story people want to see, experience, and be part of.

And now for the secret to writing Fantasy: Have fun. If you truly love what you're creating and you believe in your characters and your story, it will show in your script.

Doesn't sound different than a regular script, does it? It shouldn't. A Fantasy script has the same basic three acts that other scripts have; it has heroes and villains, roadblocks to progress, plot twists and, eventually, the resolution. There are only two differences between a Fantasy script and a non-Fantasy script: The "more" factor and magic. The magic is self-explanatory and provides fabulous pitfalls and rescues. The "more" factor was touched on in Chapter 1, What is Fantasy? Remember what I said about it? With the "more" factor, the heroes are more heroic, heroines more beautiful, quests more noble, odds more horrific. In addition, the impossible is not only possible, but plausible. I guess you could say that Fantasy is the Drama Queen of the genres.

Now that the rules, the aspirations, and the secret are out of the way, let's take a quick look at all the different elements that I've covered:

Chapter 1, What Is Fantasy? I hope this chapter has expanded the field for you and you are no longer thinking of Fantasy as just wizards, witches, heroes, and dragons. Fantasy can be anything you want it to be, so take a deep breath, reach high, and stretch your mind. Explore the many different sub-genres and find one you like, especially if this is your first try at Fantasy. I realize we should stretch our limits and try new things, but who says we can't ease into that stretch?

Chapter 2, Research: If, after this chapter you have absolutely no idea where to go for information, and you think that the subject really doesn't need to be researched, you haven't taken in a word I've written. Research is a MUST! And that's all I'll say.

Chapter 3, The Story — Part I: Remember the lesson in this chapter? — It's okay for you to come up with a story line before you come up with characters. So if you do, relax and go with it.

Chapter 4, Characters: There are as many different hero-types in Fantasy as there are in mysteries, adventure, and romance stories. When writing a character ask yourself, what is his background? Does he love? If so, whom or what? Does he hate? If so, whom or what? What are his regrets, his joys, his sorrows? Is he physically challenged? Is he loved? How do other people view him? The more you delve into his personality, the more you should ask questions.

There is no reason for a Fantasy character to be an archetype, so don't let yours slip into that trap.

Chapter 5, Beasties: As I said in this chapter, before you introduce one of these, make sure he has a purpose. Even if you have a scene in which people are being driven from their homes, they must ride or drive their livestock before them. These beasties have a purpose. They can create a comfortable feeling for an audience in an unusual place or they can heighten the strangeness into which your characters have walked.

Chapter 6, Magic: Remember that whatever type of Fantasy you are writing, there must be an element of magic to it before it can be considered a Fantasy. I strongly suggest you look beyond my little chapter on this subject and do some independent study. There is so much more to it than what we have seen in movies and TV shows.

Chapter 7, Location: YOU DON'T HAVE TO BE IN MIDDLE EUROPE! Expand your views; expand your quest for unusual stories. Explore folk stories, local and international legends, look beyond that which has been done over and over. Never stop questing for what is different; you will be well rewarded for it.

Chapter 8, Battles: Repeat after me: All battles need not be in the middle of a field with a sword in hand. And not all battles must be big and grand, or a fight between the ultimate good and evil. Battles can be small and intimate, between two people, or between man's intellect and his heart.

Chapter 9, Religion: A religious figure is not necessary in Fantasy, although there often is one. No matter what religion a character belongs to, there is a structure and code of conduct.

Chapter 10, Politics: All stories involve politics, from intimate man-woman relationships to wars between countries.

Chapter 11, Romance: More, more, more! It makes women sigh and leaves men wondering where they can get roses at midnight. It is absolutely everything you want it to be in your own life, and more, so pour your heart into it.

Chapter 12, Family: Families in Fantasy run the full spectrum of those in real life, with the added component of magic. The higher they are on the social scale, the more problems they have keeping their heads.

Chapter 13, Language: Write in your own language and suggest subtitles. Use made up (or bastardized) languages for spells.

Chapter 14, Including Music and Poetry: Leave this up to the Powers that Be, unless music and poetry play an important part in the story.

Chapter 15, Details: Remember, the Devil's in the details, do yourself a favor and take a moment to research something when you're not sure about it. You want to give your script every chance it can get to be accepted.

Chapter 16. Descriptions: Keep them concise and easy to follow. The multitude of people hired to make your vision come true can take your wildest dreams beyond your own limits.

Chapter 17, The Story — Part II: Even with the prior 16 chapters, there was still more to show, and who knows what you can find beyond this book.

Chapter 18, Putting It All Together: I have to be honest with you, this whole book is only a portion of what you can learn about taking Fantasy from prose fiction to script form. It is a genre that is so varied and so immense I can guarantee you'll never run out of material. Along with the variations and immensity are the divergent opinions about Fantasy. There are people who will read this book and think I'm an idiot and wrong in all my advice. And they'll be right. I am an idiot and all my advice is wrong... for them. But I might be right for you, or maybe part of what I've put down will be right for you. It doesn't matter. If I've made you think, if I've made you realize that Fantasy is more than what you think it is, I've served my purpose.

Fantasy is like romance, it can be everything you want it to be, if you let yourself go.

Go forth and conquer!

What They Say:
How important do you think the Fantasy genre is?

Professor Matheson:
"Very important. We tend to forget that may of the greatest and most enduring works of literature are, in fact, Fantasies. But a big distinction must be made between good Fantasy created by great imaginations (the minority) and bad Fantasy produced by "write-by-numbers" methods (the majority)."

Jim French: Author of the longest running radio detective series: *The Adventures of Harry Nile,* and producer of the radio theater Imagination Theatre for syndication and XM Satellite Radio *http://jimfrenchproductions.com.*

"I think Fantasy in any medium is always salable because reality is gritty and getting grittier. It's pleasant to relax in a universe without religious fanatics and political sleazeballs (at least of the Earth variety). All of us have Fantasy lives. I'm a believer that reading, watching and/or listening to Fantasy is a vacation for the psyche."

Any comments, in general, that you'd like to make about the state of Fantasy films (including everything from The Lord of the Rings *to* Big *and* Splash*).*

Darragh Metzger:
"Lately, I've noticed the beginnings of a trend toward holding Fantasy films (and Fantasy's sibling, Science Fiction) to the same standards as other kinds of films. This is a long-needed change, and very welcome! I hope it continues.

Too often, Fantasy films are treated like 'kid's movies,' denied the respect of 'real' art. This is in keeping with the way Fantasy novels are treated in the literary world. Tolkien is one of the very few Fantasy writers to be given the respect he deserves, and both the novel and film of *The Lord of the Rings* have, for the most part, been treated as serious works of art.

However, the more typical lack of respect given Fantasy films is also due to the fact that very few filmmakers treat Fantasy scripts with the same respect they give 'serious' works. When asked to produce a Fantasy script, most writers turn out something like *Reign of Fire*, *Scorpion King*, or *The Hulk*, because such stories are easy and familiar. Even reasonably good Fantasy movies, such as *Willow*, or *Pirates of the Caribbean* take few risks or step outside the bounds of expected formula.

It's a far greater challenge to turn out something of the quality of *The Lord of the Rings*, the new *Peter Pan*, or even *Splash*, three works that actually play with audience expectations and go outside the formula (I say this even though *The Lord of the Rings* is the source of the formula for a lot of Fantasy). Risky

Fantasy films don't always succeed — *Baron Munchhausen* and *Time Bandits* come to mind — but they can take an audience to places no other type of film can. For that alone, they need to be approached with the same degree of imagination, passion, and respect that other films are. Not as Kid's Movies, but as Art."

ABOUT THE AUTHOR

Sable Jak was born and raised in the lake country of Southern Wisconsin. She revels in memories of the sound of dragonflies buzzing and fields of butterflies rising in clouds under deep blue skies — with one or two staying behind to land on her finger. She's happy to report that butterflies still land on her fingers with regularity and she's convinced some of the shimmering wings of various bugs really belong to fairies. She also knows that someday she will step through the fairy ring, hopefully it will be at Ballynahinch. She currently resides in the Pacific Northwest, which is a near perfect climate, only slightly warmer than the perfect climate that exists in Wales.

A columnist with *Scr(i)pt Magazine's* ezine and *absolutewrite.com*, Jak is represented by EarthAngels Literary Management (representing Women and Minority Writers and Directors). Sable can be reached for consultation through her manger, Attica Peece at *attica@anet.net*.

BİBLİOGRAPHY

1. *Reference Guide to Science Fiction, Fantasy and Horror,* Burgess, Michael, Libraries Unlimited, Inc. Englewood, CO.

2. *How to Write Tales of Horror, Fantasy & Science Fiction* Writer's Digest Books, Cincinnati, OH.

3. *The Writer's Complete Fantasy Reference,* Writer's Digest Books, Cincinnati, OH.

4. *The Complete and Unabridged Bulfinch's Mythology,* Thomas Bulfinch. There are various versions from hardcover to audiocassette, and a digital download is available through *Amazon.com.*
You can also check out: *http://www.bullfinch.org/*

5. Joseph Campbell

6. *Mythology, the Illustrated Anthology of World Myth and Storytelling,* Duncan Baird Publishers, London.

7. *The Dictionary of Imaginary Places,* Alberto Manguel and Gianni Guadalupi, Harcourt.

8. *Ye Gods!*, Anne S. Baumgartner, Lyle Stuart, Inc. New Jersey.

9. *Reel People, Finding Ourselves in the Movies*, Howard M. Gluss, Ph.D., with Scott Edward Smith, Xlibris Corporation.

10. *13 Plays of Ghosts & the Supernatural selected by Marvin Kaye — Cold Journey in the Dark, A Play for Two Voices and Ideas*, Parke Goodwin, Doubleday Book & Music Clubs, Inc. New York.

11. *The Encyclopedia of Things that Never Were: Creatures, Places & People*, Michael Page, Robert Ingpen, softcover, Penguin Studio.

12. *The Encyclopedia of Fantasy*, John Clute and John Grant. Palgrave Macmillan.

13. *The Encyclopedia of Black Magic*, Mallard Press, New York.

14. *The Encyclopedia of Superstitions*, E. and M.A. Radford, Barnes and Noble Books.

15. *Encyclopedia Mysteriosa*, William L. DeAndrea, Prentice Hall, New York.

16. *Scottish Customs*, Sheila Livingtone, Barnes & Noble Books.

17. *Llewellyn's Practical Magick Series, Magical Herbalism, The Secret Craft of the Wise*, Scott Cunningham, Llewellyn Publications, St. Paul, Minnesota.

18. *A Complete Guide to Faeries & Magical Beings: Explore the Mystical Realm of the Little People*, Cassandra Eason, Red Wheel, Weiser.

19. *English Through the Ages*, William Brohaugh, Writer's Digest Books, Cincinnati, OH.

20. *Trippingly on the Tongue, A Booke of Instruction for Speaking Early Modern English*, Laura Crockett, Historical Resources.

michael wiese productions
www.mwp.com

We are delighted that you have found, and are enjoying, our books.

Since 1981, we've been all about providing filmmakers with the very best information on the craft of filmmaking: from screenwriting to funding, from directing to camera, acting, editing, distribution, and new media.

It is our goal to inspire and empower a generation (or two) of filmmakers and videomakers like yourself. But we want to go beyond providing you with just the basics. We want to shake you, inspire you to reach for your dreams, and go beyond what's been done before. Most films that come out each year waste our time and enslave our imaginations. We want to give you the confidence to create from your authentic center, to bring something from your own experience that will truly inspire others and bring humanity to its full potential — avoiding those urges to manufacture derivative work in order to be accepted.

Movies, television, the Internet, and new media all have incredible power to transform. As you prepare your next project, know that it is in your hands to choose to create something magnificent and enduring for generations to come.

This is not an impossible goal, because you've got a little help. Our authors are some of the most creative mentors in the business, willing to share their hard-earned insights with you. Their books will point you in the right direction but, ultimately, it's up to you to seek that authentic something on which to spend your precious time.

We applaud your efforts and are here to support you. Let us hear from you.

Sincerely,

Michael Wiese
Filmmaker, Publisher

WRITING THE COMEDY FILM
Make 'Em Laugh

Stuart Voytilla and Scott Petri

In *Myth and the Movies*, Stuart Voytilla introduced how mythic structure can help us understand the characteristics of any genre. Now Voytilla and Petri take you deeper into the special world of crafting memorable genre stories. Writing for genre isn't "plug-in-play" formulas and "paint-by-the-numbers" characters but developing an awareness and appreciation of genre conventions and audience expectations. This concise, easy-to-use guidebook — packed with extensive examples from classic film and exercises for developing craft — will help writers of all levels learn the secrets of genre as seen through the powerful lens of myth and archetype.

A writer and literary consultant, Stuart Voytilla also teaches screenwriting and film aesthetics at San Diego State University. Scott Petri is an award-winning humorist who has authored or co-authored 12 screenplays.

$14.95 | 180 pages | Order # 106RLS | ISBN:0-941188-41-8

THE CRIME WRITER'S
COMPLETE REFERENCE GUIDE
1001 Tips for Writing
the Perfect Crime

Martin Roth

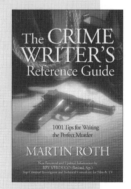

New foreword and updated information by Sgt. Rey Verdugo, Top Criminal Investigator and Technical Consultant for Film & TV

Here's the book no writer of murder mysteries, thrillers, action-adventure, true crime, police procedurals, romantic suspense, and psychological mysteries — whether scripts or novels — can do without. Martin Roth provides all the particulars to make your crime story accurate.

$17.95 | 300 pages | Order # 105RLS | ISBN: 0-941188-49-3

SCREENWRITING 101
The Essential Craft
of Feature Film Writing

Neill D. Hicks

Hicks brings the clarity and practical instruction familiar to his students and readers to screenwriters everywhere. In his inimitable and colorful style, he tells the beginning screenwriter how the mechanics of Hollywood storytelling work, and how to use those elements to create a script with blockbuster potential without falling into clichés.

Neill D. Hicks' screenwriting credits include *Rumble in the Bronx* and *First Strike*.

$16.95 | 220 pages | Order # 41RLS | ISBN: 0-941188-72-8

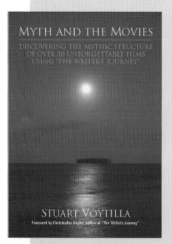

MYTH AND THE MOVIES
Discovering the Mythic
Structure of 50
Unforgettable Films

Stuart Voytilla
Foreword by Christopher Vogler
Author of *The Writer's Journey*

An illuminating companion piece to *The Writer's Journey*, *Myth and the Movies* applies the mythic structure Vogler developed to 50 well-loved U.S. and foreign films. This comprehensive book offers a greater understanding of why some films continue to touch and connect with audiences generation after generation.

Movies discussed include *Die Hard*, *Singin' in the Rain*, *Boyz N the Hood*, *Pulp Fiction*, *The Searchers*, *La Strada*, and *The Silence of the Lambs*.

Stuart Voytilla is a writer, script consultant, and teacher of acting and screenwriting and the co-author of *Writing the Comedy Film*.

$26.95 | 300 pages | Order # 39RLS | ISBN: 0-941188-66-3

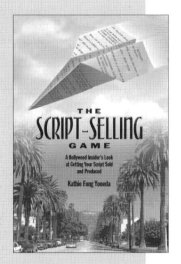

WRITING THE
ACTION-ADVENTURE FILM
The Moment of Truth

Neill D. Hicks

The Action-Adventure movie is consistently one of the most popular exports of the American film industry, drawing enormous audiences worldwide across many diverse societies, cultures, and languages.

But there are more than hot pursuits, hot lead, and hot-headed slugfests in a successful Action-Adventure script. With definitive examples from over 100 movies, *Writing the Action-Adventure Film* reveals the screenwriting principles that define the content and the style of this popular film genre. Neill Hicks furnishes a set of tools to build a compelling screenplay that fulfills the expectations of the motion picture audience.

$14.95 | 180 pages | Order # 99RLS | ISBN: 0-941188-39-6

WRITING
THE THRILLER FILM
The Terror Within

Neill D. Hicks

A good Thriller will rupture the reality of your everyday world. It will put you on guard. Make you *aware*. That is the disquieting objective — successfully achieved — of this book as well.

Writing the Thriller Film concentrates on the Cosmos of Credibility, those not-so-obvious elements of screenwriting that contribute the essential meaning to a script. To do so, this book traces the thematic commonalities that actually define the genre, and offers corroboration from a number of screenplays, including such classics as *North by Northwest*, *Marathon Man*, and *3 Days of the Condor*.

$14.95 | 168 pages | Order # 101RLS | ISBN: 0-941188-46-9

STEALING FIRE FROM THE GODS
A Dynamic New Story Model
for Writers and Filmmakers

James Bonnet

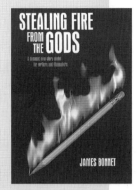

In the tradition of Carl Jung, Joseph Campbell, and Christopher Vogler, James Bonnet explores the connection between mythic storytelling and personal growth. *Stealing Fire From the Gods* investigates the elements that make traditional tales so enduring, and shows how modern writers can use those same elements to make their own stories more powerful, memorable, and emotionally resonant.

James Bonnet, founder of Astoria Filmwrights, is a successful screen and television writer who has been elected twice to the Board of Directors of the Writers Guild.

$26.95 | 235 pages | Order # 38RLS | ISBN: 0-941188-65-5

WRITING THE SECOND ACT
Building Conflict and
Tension in Your Film Script

Michael Halperin

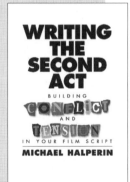

Every screenplay needs an attention-grabbing beginning and a satisfying ending, but the second act is the meat of your story, where your characters grow, change, and overcome the obstacles that will bring them to the resolution at the end of the story. Consequently, it's also the hardest act to write, and where most screenplays tend to lose momentum and focus. This book will help writers through that crucial 60-page stretch. Structural elements and plot devices are discussed in detail, as well as how to keep the action moving and the characters evolving while the audience stays wrapped up in your story.

$19.95 | 161 Pages | Order # 49RLS | ISBN: 0-941188-29-9

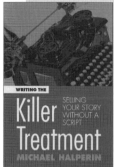

WRITING THE KILLER TREATMENT
Selling Your Story without a Script

Michael Halperin

The most commonly heard phrase in Hollywood is not "Let's do lunch." In reality, the expression you'll most often hear in production, studio, and agency offices is: "Okay, send me a treatment."

A treatment, which may range from one to several dozen pages, is the snapshot of your feature film or TV script. A treatment reveals your story's structure, introduces your characters and hooks, and is often your first and only opportunity to pitch your project.

This is the only book that takes you through the complete process of creating treatments that sell. It includes: developing believable characters and story structure; understanding the distinctions between treatments for screenplays, adaptations, sitcoms, Movies of the Week, episodic television, and soaps; useful exercises that will help you develop your craft as a writer; insightful interviews with Oscar and Emmy winners; tips and query letters for finding an agent and/or a producer; and *What Every Writer Needs to Know*, from the Writers Guild of America, west.

$14.95 | 171 pages | Order # 97RLS | ISBN: 0-941188-40-X

THE WRITER'S PARTNER
1001 Breakthrough Ideas
to Stimulate Your Imagination

Martin Roth

This book is the complete source, as reliable and indispensable as its title implies. Whether you're looking for inspiration for new plotlines and characters or need help fleshing out your characters and settings with depth, detail, color, and texture, Martin Roth will turn your script into a strong, memorable work. This comprehensive classic covers every major genre, from action to suspense to comedy to romance to horror. With *The Writer's Partner*, you'll feel like you're in a roomful of talented writers helping you to perfect your screenplay!

$19.95 | 349 pages | Order # 3RLS | ISBN: 0-941188-32-9

FILM DIRECTING: SHOT BY SHOT
Visualizing from
Concept to Screen

film directing
shot by shot
visualizing from concept to screen

Steven D. Katz

Over 160,000 Sold! International best-seller!

Film Directing: Shot by Shot — with its famous blue cover — is the best-known book on directing and a favorite of professional directors as an on-set quick reference guide.

This international bestseller is a complete catalog of visual techniques and their stylistic implications, enabling working filmmakers to expand their knowledge.

Contains in-depth information on shot composition, staging sequences, visualization tools, framing and composition techniques, camera movement, blocking tracking shots, script analysis, and much more.

Includes over 750 storyboards and illustrations, with never-before-published storyboards from Steven Spielberg's *Empire of the Sun*, Orson Welles' *Citizen Kane*, and Alfred Hitchcock's *The Birds*.

"(To become a director) you have to teach yourself what makes movies good and what makes them bad. John Singleton has been my mentor... he's the one who told me what movies to watch and to read *Shot by Shot*."
— Ice Cube, *New York Times*

"A generous number of photos and superb illustrations accompany each concept, many of the graphics being from Katz' own pen... *Film Directing: Shot by Shot* is a feast for the eyes."
— *Videomaker Magazine*

Steven D. Katz is also the author of *Film Directing: Cinematic Motion*.

$27.95 | 366 pages | Order # 7RLS | ISBN: 0-941188-10-8

ORDER FORM

TO ORDER THESE PRODUCTS, PLEASE CALL 24 HOURS - 7 DAYS A WEEK
CREDIT CARD ORDERS 1-800-833-5738 OR FAX YOUR ORDER (818) 986-3408
OR MAIL THIS ORDER FORM TO:

MICHAEL WIESE PRODUCTIONS
11288 VENTURA BLVD., # 621
STUDIO CITY, CA 91604
E-MAIL: MWPSALES@MWP.COM
WEB SITE: WWW.MWP.COM

WRITE OR FAX FOR A FREE CATALOG

PLEASE SEND ME THE FOLLOWING BOOKS:

TITLE	ORDER NUMBER (#RLS _____)	AMOUNT

SHIPPING _____

CALIFORNIA TAX (8.00%) _____

TOTAL ENCLOSED _____

SHIPPING:
ALL ORDERS MUST BE PREPAID, UPS GROUND SERVICE ONE ITEM - $3.95
EACH ADDITIONAL ITEM ADD $2.00
EXPRESS - 3 BUSINESS DAYS ADD $12.00 PER ORDER
OVERSEAS
SURFACE - $15.00 EACH ITEM   AIRMAIL - $30.00 EACH ITEM

PLEASE MAKE CHECK OR MONEY ORDER PAYABLE TO:

MICHAEL WIESE PRODUCTIONS

(CHECK ONE) ____ MASTERCARD ____VISA ____AMEX

CREDIT CARD NUMBER _____

EXPIRATION DATE _____

CARDHOLDER'S NAME _____

CARDHOLDER'S SIGNATURE _____

SHIP TO:

NAME _____

ADDRESS _____

CITY _____ STATE _____ ZIP _____

COUNTRY _____ TELEPHONE _____

ORDER ONLINE FOR THE LOWEST PRICES

24 HOURS | 1.800.833.5738 | www.mwp.com